50 Leveled Math Problems

Level

150 Problems Total

Author

Linda Dacey, Ed.D.

 **Lesley** UNIVERSITY

 **SHELL EDUCATION**

Contributing Author and Consultant

Anne M. Collins, Ph.D.
Director of Mathematics Programs
Director of Achievement Center
  for Mathematics
Lesley University

Consultants

Jayne Bamford Lynch, M.Ed.
National Faculty
Lesley University

Johanny Canada-Hlatshwayo
Mathematics Coach
Cambridge Public Schools

Corinne Varion-Green, Ed.D.
Teacher, Grade 2
Cambridge Public Schools

Carolyn McElligott, M.Ed.
Teacher, Grade 2
Winthrop School, Melrose, MA

Publishing Credits

Dona Herweck Rice, *Editor-in-Chief;* Robin Erickson, *Production Director;* Lee Aucoin, *Creative Director;* Timothy J. Bradley, *Illustration Manager;* Sara Johnson, M.S.Ed., *Senior Editor;* Aubrie Nielsen, M.S.Ed., *Associate Education Editor;* Leah Quillian, *Assistant Editor;* Grace Alba, *Interior Layout Designer;* Corinne Burton, M.A.Ed., *Publisher*

Standards
© 2003 National Council of Teachers of Mathematics (NCTM)
© 2004 Mid-continent Research for Education and Learning (McREL)
© 2007 Teachers of English to Speakers of Other Languages, Inc. (TESOL)
© 2010 National Governors Association Center for Best Practices and Council of Chief State School Officers

Shell Education
5301 Oceanus Drive
Huntington Beach, CA 92649-1030
http://www.shelleducation.com
ISBN 978-1-4258-0774-0
© 2012 Shell Educational Publishing, Inc.
Reprinted 2013

Table of Contents

Introduction

Leveled Problem-Solving Lessons

Operations and Algebraic Thinking

Number and Operations in Base Ten

Table of Contents *(cont.)*

Problem Solving in Mathematics Instruction

If you were a student in elementary school before the early 1980s, your education most likely paid little or no attention to mathematical problem solving. In fact, your exposure may have been limited to solving word problems at the end of a chapter that focused on one of the four operations. After a chapter on addition, for example, you solved problems that required you to add two numbers to find the answer. You knew this was the case, so you just picked out the two numbers from the problem and added them. Sometimes, but rarely, you were assigned problems that required you to choose whether to add, subtract, multiply, or divide. Many of your teachers dreaded lessons that contained such problems as they did not know how to help the many students who struggled.

If you went to elementary school in the later 1980s or in the 1990s, it may have been different. You may have learned about a four-step model of problem solving and perhaps you were introduced to different strategies for finding solutions. There may have been a separate chapter in your textbook that focused on problem solving and two-page lessons that focused on particular problem-solving strategies, such as guess and check. Attention was given to problems that required more than one computational step for their solution, and all the information necessary to solve the problems was not necessarily contained in the problem statements.

One would think that the ability of students to solve problems would improve greatly with these changes, but that has not been the case. Research provides little evidence that teaching problem solving in this isolated manner leads to success (Cai 2010). In fact, some would argue that valuable instructional time was lost exploring problems that did not match the mathematical goals of the curriculum. An example would be learning how to use logic tables to solve a problem that involved finding out who drank which drink and wore which color shirt. Being able to use a diagram to organize information, to reason deductively, and to eliminate possibilities are all important problem-solving skills, but they should be applied to problems that are mathematically significant and interesting to students.

Today, leaders in mathematics education recommend teaching mathematics in a manner that integrates attention to concepts, skills, and mathematical reasoning. Referred to as *teaching through problem solving*, this approach suggests that problematic tasks serve as vehicles through which students acquire new mathematical concepts and skills (D'Ambrosio 2003). Students apply previous learning and gain new insights into mathematics as they wrestle with challenging tasks. This approach is quite different from introducing problems only after content has been learned.

Most recently, the *Common Core State Standards* listed the need to persevere in problem solving as the first of its Standards for Mathematical Practice (National Governors Association Center for Best Practices and Council of Chief State School Officers 2010):

> **Make sense of problems and persevere in solving them.**
>
> *Mathematically proficient students start by explaining to themselves the meaning of a problem and looking for entry points to its solution. They analyze givens, constraints, relationships, and goals. They make conjectures about the form and meaning of the solution and plan a solution pathway rather than simply jumping into a solution attempt. They consider analogous problems, and try special cases and simpler forms of the original problem in order to*

Problem Solving in Mathematics Instruction *(cont.)*

gain insight into its solution. They monitor and evaluate their progress and change course if necessary. Older students might, depending on the context of the problem, transform algebraic expressions or change the viewing window on their graphing calculator to get the information they need. Mathematically proficient students can explain correspondences between equations, verbal descriptions, tables, and graphs or draw diagrams of important features and relationships, graph data, and search for regularity or trends. Younger students might rely on using concrete objects or pictures to help conceptualize and solve a problem. Mathematically proficient students check their answers to problems using a different method, and they continually ask themselves, "Does this make sense?" They can understand the approaches of others to solving complex problems and identify correspondences between different approaches.

This sustained commitment to problem solving makes sense; it is the application of mathematical skills to real-life problems that makes learning mathematics so important. Unfortunately, we have not yet mastered the art of developing successful problem solvers. Students' performance in the United States on the 2009 Program for International Student Assessment (PISA), a test that evaluates 15-year-old students' mathematical literacy and ability to apply mathematics to real-life situations, suggests that we need to continue to improve our teaching of mathematical problem solving. According to data released late in 2010, students in the U.S. are below average (National Center for Educational Statistics 2010). Clearly we need to address this lack of success.

Students do not have enough opportunities to solve challenging problems. Further, problems available to teachers are not designed to meet the individual needs of students. Additionally, teachers have few opportunities to learn how best to create, identify, and orchestrate problem-solving tasks. *50 Leveled Math Problems* is a unique series that is designed to address these concerns.

Understanding the Problem-Solving Process

George Polya is known as the father of problem solving. In his book *How to Solve It: A New Aspect of Mathematical Method* (1945), Polya provides a four-step model of problem solving that has been adopted in many classrooms: understanding the problem, making a plan, carrying out the plan, and looking back. In some elementary classrooms this model has been shortened to: understand, plan, do, check. Unfortunately, this over-simplification ignores much of the richness of Polya's thinking.

Polya's conceptual model of the problem-solving process has been adapted for use at this level. Teachers are encouraged to view the four steps as interrelated, rather than only sequential, and to recognize that problem-solving strategies are useful at each stage of the problem-solving process. The model presented here gives greater emphasis to the importance of communicating and justifying one's thinking as well as to posing problems. Ways in which understanding is deepened throughout the problem-solving process are considered in each of the following steps.

Step 1: Understand the Problem

Students engage in the problem-solving process when they attempt to understand the problem, but the understanding is not something that just happens in the beginning. At grade 2 the teacher or the students may read the problem aloud. Students may be asked to restate the problem in their own words and then turn to a partner to summarize what they know and what they need to find out. At this grade level, it is important for students to be able to visualize or model the problem.

What is most important is that teachers do not teach students to rely on key words or show students "tricks" or "short-cuts" that are not built on conceptual understanding. Interpreting the language of mathematics is complex, and terms that are used in mathematics often have different everyday meanings. Note how a reliance on key words would lead to failure when solving the following problem. A student taught that *left* means *subtract* may decide that 10 – 6, or 4 steps, is the correct answer.

Melissa walked 10 steps.

Then she turned to the left and walked 6 more steps.

Understanding the Problem-Solving Process (cont.)

Step 2: Apply Strategies

Once students have a sense of the problem they can begin to actively explore it. They may do so by applying one or more of the strategies below. Note that related actions are combined within some of the strategies.

- Act it out or use manipulatives.
- Count, compute, or write an equation.
- Find information in a picture, list, table, graph, or diagram.
- Generalize a pattern.
- Guess and check or make an estimate.

- Organize information in a picture, list, table, graph, or diagram.
- Simplify the problem.
- Use logical reasoning.
- Work backward.

As students apply these strategies, they also deepen their understanding of the *mathematics* of the problem. As such, understanding develops throughout the problem-solving phases. Consider the following problem and scenario requiring students to write the numbers in the blanks so that the story makes sense.

Jamie held _____ animals at the pet store.
            A

A= _____

She held mice, hamsters, and guinea pigs at the pet store.

B= _____

She held _____ more guinea pigs than mice.
            B

C= _____

Jamie held _____ guinea pigs and _____
            C   D

D= _____

mice. Jamie also held _____ hamsters.
                        E

E= _____

Pia and Richard are working together. They have read the problem and understand that they are to write numbers so that the story makes sense. When Richard says, "We can just write any numbers we want. This is easy!" Pia responds, "Okay, let's do it." She writes a 6 in the first blank and Richard writes a 10 in the next one. Then Pia says, "Wait, we can't have 10 guinea pigs and only 6 animals." By making a guess and checking it, Pia and Richard came to understand the necessary relationship among the numbers they wrote and the related information in the text.

It is important that we offer students problems that can be solved in more than one way. If one strategy does not lead to success, students can try a different one. This option gives students the opportunity to learn that getting "stuck" might just mean that a new approach should be considered. When students get themselves "unstuck" they are more likely to view themselves as successful problem solvers. Such problems also lead to richer mathematical conversations as there are different ideas and perspectives to discuss.

Understanding the Problem-Solving Process *(cont.)*

Step 2: Apply Strategies *(cont.)*

Consider the following problem:

> *There are 4 bags of fruit.*
>
> *There are 2 bananas and 2 apples in each bag.*
>
> *What is the total number of pieces of fruit in these bags?*

Reflect on the student responses below. In Student Sample 1, the student begins by drawing a picture of the apples and bananas, records the four under each bag, and then combines two sets of fours to find that 8 + 8 = 16. For her written explanation, she focused on the importance of fours in the problem.

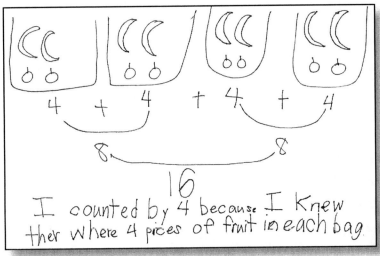

Student Sample 1

In Student Sample 2, the student begins in a similar manner, drawing the apples and bananas in each bag. He then documents how he can add by fours, twos, or ones to get the answer of sixteen pieces of fruit. His written statement summarizes these possibilities and suggests a connection between counting and addition.

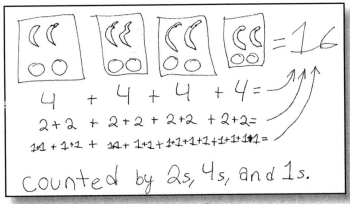

Student Sample 2

Understanding the Problem-Solving Process *(cont.)*

Step 2: Apply Strategies *(cont.)*

As the student did in Student Sample 3, some students may recognize that the equal groups suggest multiplication. Note that she also records the number in each group, rather than making a drawing.

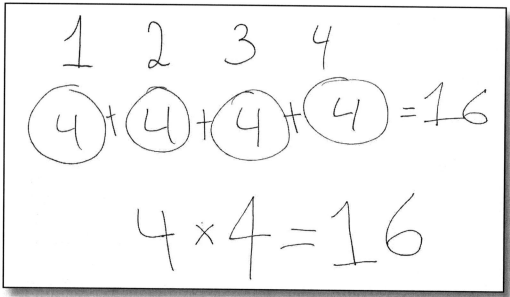

Student Sample 3

Step 3: Communicate and Justify Your Thinking

It is essential that teachers ask students to communicate and justify their thinking. It is also important that students make records as they work so that they can recall their thinking. When teachers make it clear that they expect such behavior from students, they are establishing an important habit of mind (Goldenberg, Shteingold, and Feurzeig 2003) and developing their understanding of the nature of mathematics. When students explain their thinking orally while investigating a problem with a partner or small group, they may deepen their understanding of the problem or recognize an error and fix it. When students debrief after finding solutions, they learn to communicate their thinking clearly and in ways that give others access to new mathematical ideas. In one class a second-grader listened to a peer's explanation and proclaimed, "So you made a number line to figure it out. I'm going to try that." Such discourse is essential to the mathematical practice suggested in the *Common Core State Standards* that students "construct viable justifications and critique the reasoning of others" (National Governors Association Center for Best Practices and Council of Chief State School Officers 2010).

Our task is to foster learning environments where students engage in this kind of *accountable talk*. Michaels, O'Connor, and Resnick (2008) identify three aspects of this type of dialogue. The first is that students are accountable to their learning communities; they listen to each other carefully and build on the ideas of others. Second, accountable talk is based on logical thinking and leads to logical conclusions. Finally, these types of discussions are based on facts or other information that is available to everyone.

Understanding the Problem-Solving Process *(cont.)*

Step 3: Communicate and Justify Your Thinking *(cont.)*

When we emphasize the importance of discussions and explanations, we are teaching our students that it is the soundness of their mathematical reasoning that determines what is correct, not merely an answer key or a teacher's approval. Students learn, therefore, that mathematics makes sense and that they are mathematical sense-makers.

Step 4: Take It Further

Debrief

It is this final step in the problem-solving process to which teachers and students are most likely to give the least attention. When time is given to this step, it is often limited to "check your work." In contrast, this step offers rich opportunities for further learning. Students might be asked to solve the problem using a different strategy, or to find additional solutions. They might be asked to make a mathematical generalization based on their investigation. Students might connect this problem to another problem they have solved already, or they now may be able to solve a new, higher-level problem. Second-grade teacher Carolyn McElligott supports the idea that students can debrief together after solving different problems:

> *I would usually describe myself as a teacher who is pretty good at differentiating my math lessons. Typically, the range of learners in my classroom is within my reach. This year, however, I have been challenged to meet all their needs, as the range is greater than usual. Close to half of my students are not meeting grade-level expectations and require extra support on a daily basis. I have struggled with managing my class to accommodate their needs while extending the thinking of my other students.*
>
> *Using leveled problems this year has allowed me to focus on the same mathematical goals while still providing just the right problem for each level of learner. What was most insightful to me was how independent the students became when the problems were best suited for their mathematical understandings. Surprisingly, this provided me time to meet with small groups of children who needed additional direct instruction.*
>
> *Working on the problems in the lesson* Living on Main Street [page 68], *my students were able to share their strategies in a large group discussion even though they solved different problems. Crossing out numbers as they did not fit the clues was the universal strategy that all of the levels seemed to have in common. Using number lines to represent the range of numbers provided by the clues was a new model that was used by two partner pairs, but could be tried by all. Students gave thumbs up when asked if they would be willing to try this model. Sharing these problems together gave all children access to the vocabulary presented as well as an appreciation for new strategies they could try.*

Understanding the Problem-Solving Process *(cont.)*

Step 4: Take It Further *(cont.)*

Posing Problems

Students can also take problem solving further by posing problems. In fact, problem posing is intricately linked with problem solving (Brown and Walter 2005). When posing their own problems, students can view a problem as something they can create, rather than as a task that is given to them. This book supports problem posing through a variety of formats. For example, students may be asked to supply missing data in a problem so that it makes sense. They may be given a problem with the question omitted and asked to compose one. Or, they may be given both problem data and the answer and asked to identify the missing question. Teachers may also choose to ask students to create their own problems similar to those they have previously solved. Emphasis on problem posing can transform the teaching of problem solving and build lifelong curiosity in students.

#50774—50 Leveled Math Problems, Level 2

Problem-Solving Strategies

Think of someone doing repair jobs around the house. Often that person carries a toolbox or wears a tool belt from task to task. Common tools such as hammers, screwdrivers, and wrenches are then readily available. The repair person chooses tools (usually more than one) appropriate for a particular task. Problem-solving strategies are the tools used to solve problems. Labeling the strategies allows students to refer to them in discussions and helps students recognize the wide variety of tools available for the solution of problems. The problems in this book provide opportunities for students to apply one or more of the following strategies:

Act It Out or Use Manipulatives

Students' understanding of a problem is greatly enhanced when they act it out. Students may choose to dramatize a situation themselves or use manipulatives to show the actions or changes that take place. If students suggest they do not understand a problem say something such as *Imagine this is a play. Show me what the actors are doing.*

Count, Compute, or Write an Equation

When students count, compute, or write an equation to solve a problem they are making a match between a context and a mathematical skill. Once the connection is made, students need only to carry out the procedure accurately. Sometimes writing an equation is a final step in the solution process. For example, students might work with manipulatives or draw pictures and then summarize their thinking by recording an equation.

Find Information in a Picture, List, Table, Graph, or Diagram

Too often problems contain all of the necessary information in the problem statement. Such information is never so readily available in real-world situations. It is important that students develop the ability to interpret a picture, list, table, graph, or diagram and identify the information relevant to the problem.

Generalize a Pattern

Some people consider mathematics the study of patterns, so it makes sense that the ability to identify, continue, and generalize patterns is an important problem-solving strategy. The ability to generalize a pattern requires students to recognize and express relationships. Once generalized, the student can use the pattern to predict other outcomes.

Guess and Check or Make an Estimate

Guessing and checking or making an estimate provide students with insights into problems. Making a guess can help students to better understand conditions of the problem; it can be a way to try something when a student is stuck. Some students may make random guesses, but over time, students learn to make more informed guesses. For example, if a guess leads to an answer that is too large, a student might next try a number that is less than the previous guess. Estimation can help students narrow their range of guesses or be used to check a guess.

Problem-Solving Strategies *(cont.)*

Organize Information in a Picture, List, Table, Graph, or Diagram

Organizing information can help students both understand and solve problems. For example, students might draw a number line or a map to note information given in the problem statement. When students organize data in a table or graph they might recognize relationships among the data. Students might also make an organized list to keep track of guesses they have made or to identify patterns. It is important that students gather data from a problem and organize it in a way that makes the most sense to them.

Simplify the Problem

Another way for students to better understand a problem, or perhaps get "unstuck," is to simplify it. Often the easiest way for students to do this is to make the numbers easier. For example, a student might replace four-digit numbers with single-digit numbers or replace fractions with whole numbers. With simpler numbers students often gain insights or recognize relationships that were not previously apparent, but that can now be applied to the original problem. Students might also work with 10 numbers, rather than 100, to identify patterns.

Use Logical Reasoning

Logical thinking and sense-making pervade mathematical problem solving. To solve problems students need to deduce relationships, draw conclusions, make inferences, and eliminate possibilities. Logical reasoning is also a component of many other strategies. For example, students use logical reasoning to revise initial guesses or to interpret diagrams. Asking questions such as *What else does this sentence tell you?* helps students to more closely analyze given data.

Work Backward

When the outcome of a situation is known, we often work backward to determine how to arrive at that goal. We might use this strategy to figure out what time to leave for the airport when we know the time our flight is scheduled to depart. A student might work backward to answer the question *What did Joey add to 79 to get a sum of 146?* or *If it took 2 hours and 23 minutes to drive a given route and the driver arrived at 10:17, at what time did the driver leave home?* Understanding relationships among the operations is critical to the successful use of this strategy.

Ask, Don't Tell

All teachers want their students to succeed, and it can be difficult to watch them struggle. Often when students struggle with a problem, a first instinct may be to step in and show them how to solve it. That intervention might feel good, but it is not helpful to the student. Students need to learn how to struggle through the problem-solving process if they are to enhance their understanding and reasoning skills. Perseverance in solving problems is listed under the mathematical practices in the *Common Core State Standards* and research indicates that students who struggle and persevere in solving problems are more likely to internalize the problem-solving process and build upon their successes. It is also important to recognize the fact that people think differently about how to approach and solve problems.

An effective substitution for telling or showing students how to solve problems is to offer support through questioning. George Bright and Jeane Joyner (2005) identify three different types of questions to ask, depending on where students are in the problem-solving process: (1) engaging questions, (2) refocusing questions, and (3) clarifying questions.

Engaging Questions

Engaging questions are designed to pique student interest in a problem. Students are more likely to want to solve problems that are interesting and relevant. One way to immediately grab a student's attention is by using his or her name in the problem. Once a personal connection is made, a student is more apt to persevere in solving the problem. Posing an engaging question is also a great way to redirect a student who is not involved in a group discussion. Suppose students are provided the missing numbers in a problem and one of the sentences reads *Janel is about _____ centimeters tall and rides her bicycle to school.* Engaging questions might include *What do you know about 100 centimeters? Are you taller or shorter than 100 centimeters?* The responses will provide further insight into how the student is thinking.

Refocusing Questions

Refocusing questions are asked to redirect students away from a nonproductive line of thinking and back to a more appropriate track. These questions often begin with the phrase *What can you tell me about…?* or *What does this number…?* Refocusing questions are also appropriate if you suspect students have misread or misunderstood the problem. Asking them to explain in their own words what the problem is stating and what question they are trying to answer is often helpful.

Clarifying Questions

Clarifying questions are posed when it is unclear why students have used a certain strategy, picture, table, graph, or computation. They are designed to help demonstrate what students are thinking, but can also be used to clear up misconceptions students might have. The teacher might say *I am not sure why you started with the number 10. Can you explain that to me?*

As teachers transform instruction from "teaching as telling" to "teaching as facilitating," students may require an adjustment period to become accustomed to the change in expectations. Over time, students will learn to take more responsibility and to expect the teacher to probe their thinking, rather than supply them with answers. After making this transition in her own teaching, one teacher shared a student's comment: "I know when I ask you a question that you are only going to ask me a question in response. But, sometimes the question helps me figure out the next step I need to take. I like that."

Differentiating with Leveled Problems

There are four main ways that teachers can differentiate: by content, by process, by product, and by learning environment. Differentiation by content involves varying the material that is presented to students. Differentiation by process occurs when a teacher delivers instruction to students in different ways. Differentiation by product asks students to present their work in different ways. Offering different learning environments, such as small group settings, is another method of differentiation. Students' learning styles, readiness levels, and interests determine which differentiation strategies are implemented. The leveled problems in this book vary aspects of mathematics problems so that students at various readiness levels can succeed. Mini-lessons include problems at three levels and ideas for differentiation. These are designated by the following symbols:

⬤ lower-level challenge

▢ on-level challenge

△ above-level challenge

☆ English language learner support

Ideally, students solve problems that are at just the right level of challenge—beyond what would be too easy, but not so difficult as to cause extreme frustration (Sylwester 2003; Tomlinson 2003; Vygotsky 1986). The goal is to avoid both a lack of challenge, which might leave students bored, as well as too much of a challenge, which might lead to significant anxiety.

There are a variety of ways to level problems. In this book, problems are leveled based on the concepts and skills required to find the solution. Problems are leveled by adjusting one or more of the following factors:

Complexity of the Mathematical Language

The mathematical language used in problems can have a significant impact on their level of challenge. For example, the term *more* is easier for students to understand than the term *less*. So a problem that states that there are *more than* 7 is simpler to understand than one stating that there are *less than 12*. An even more complex phrase would be *at least 7*.

Complexity of the Task

There are various ways to change the complexity of the task. One example would be the number of solutions that students are expected to identify. Finding one solution that satisfies problem conditions is less challenging than finding more than one solution, which is even less difficult than identifying *all* possible solutions. Similarly, increases and decreases in the number of conditions that must be met and the number of steps that must be completed change the complexity of a problem.

Differentiating with Leveled Problems *(cont.)*

Changing the Numbers

Sometimes it is the size of the numbers that is changed to increase the level of mathematical skills required. A problem may be more complex when it involves three-digit numbers rather than two-digit numbers. Sometimes changes to the "friendliness" of the numbers are made to adapt the difficulty level. For example, if students need to find the total of three one-digit numbers and two of them sum to ten, the task will be easier than if no two numbers sum to ten.

Amount of Support

Some problems provide more support for learners than others. Providing a graphic organizer or a table that is partially completed is one way to provide added support for students. Offering information with pictures rather than words can also vary the level of support. The inclusion of such supports often helps students to better understand problems and may offer insights on how to proceed. The exclusion of supports allows a learner to take more responsibility for finding a solution, and it may make the task appear more abstract or challenging.

Differentiation Strategies for English Language Learners

Many English language learners may work at a high readiness level in many mathematical concepts, but may need support in accessing the language content. Specific suggestions for differentiating for English language learners can be found in the *Differentiate* section of some mini-lessons. Additionally, the strategies below may assist teachers in differentiating for English language learners.

- Allow students to draw pictures or provide oral responses as an alternative to written responses.
- Pose questions with question stems or frames. Example question stems/frames include:
  - *What would happen if…?*,
  - *Why do you think…?*,
  - *How would you prove…?*,
  - *How is _____ related to _____?*, and
  - *Why is _____ important?*
- Use visuals to give context to questions. Add pictures or icons next to key words, or use realia to help students understand the scenario of the problem.
- Provide sentence stems or frames to help students articulate their thoughts. Sentence stems include:
  - *This is important because…*,
  - *This is similar because…*, and
  - *This is different because….*

  Sentence frames include:
  - *I agree with _____ because…*,
  - *I disagree with _____ because…*, and
  - *I think _____ because….*
- Partner English language learners with language-proficient students.

Management and Assessment

Organization of the Mini-Lessons

The mini-lessons in this book are organized according to the domains identified in the *Common Core State Standards*, which have also been endorsed by the National Council of Teachers of Mathematics. At grade 2, these domains are *Operations and Algebraic Thinking, Number and Operations in Base Ten, Measurement and Data,* and *Geometry.* Though organized in this manner, the mini-lessons are independent of one another and may be taught in any order within a domain or among the domains. What is most important is that the lessons are implemented in the order that best fits a teacher's curriculum and practice.

Ways to Use the Mini-Lessons

There are a variety of ways to assign and use the mini-lessons, and they may be implemented in different ways throughout the year. The lessons can provide practice with new concepts or be used to maintain skills previously learned. The problems can be incorporated into a teacher's mathematics lessons once or twice each week, or they may be used to introduce extended or additional instructional periods. They can be used in the regular classroom with the whole class or in small groups. They can also be used to support Response to Intervention (RTI) and after-school programs.

It is important to remember that a student's ability to solve problems depends greatly on the specific content involved and may change over the course of the school year. Establish the expectation that problem assignment is flexible; sometimes students will be assigned to one level (circle, square, or triangle) and sometimes to another. On occasion, you may also wish to allow students to choose their own problems. Much can be learned from students' choices!

Students can also be assigned one, two, or all three of the problems to solve. Although leveled, some students who are capable of wrestling with complex problems need the opportunity to warm up first to build their confidence. Starting at a lower level serves these students well. Teachers may also find that students correctly assigned to a below- or on-level problem will be able to consider a problem at a higher level after solving one of the lower problems. Students can also revisit these problems, investigating those at the higher levels not previously explored.

Grouping Students to Solve Leveled Problems

A differentiated classroom often groups students in a variety of ways, based on the instructional goals of an activity or the tasks students must complete. At times, students may work in heterogeneous groups or pairs with students of varying readiness levels. Other activities may lend themselves to homogeneous groups or pairs of students who share similar readiness levels. Since the problems presented in this book provide below-level, on-level, and above-level challenges, you may wish to partner or group students with others who are working at the same readiness level.

Since students' readiness levels may vary for different mathematical concepts and change throughout a course of study, students may be assigned different levels of problems at different times throughout

Management and Assessment *(cont.)*

Grouping Students to Solve Leveled Problems *(cont.)*

the year (or even throughout a week). It is important that the grouping of students for solving leveled problems stay flexible. Struggling students who feel that they are constantly assigned to work with a certain partner or group may develop feelings of shame or stigma. Above-level students who are routinely assigned to the same group may become disinterested and cause behavior problems. Varying students' groups can help keep the activities interesting and engaging.

Assessment for Learning

In recent years, increased attention has been given to summative assessment in schools. Significantly more instructional time is taken with weekly quizzes, chapter tests, and state-mandated assessments. These tests, although seen as tedious by many, provide information and reports about achievement to students, parents, administrators, and other interested stakeholders. However, these summative assessments often do not have a real impact on an individual student's learning. In fact, when teachers return quizzes and tests, many students look at the grade, and if it is "good," they bring the assessment home. If it is not an acceptable grade, they often just throw away the assessment.

Research shows that to have an impact on student learning we should rely on assessments *for* learning, rather than assessments *of* learning. That is, we should focus on assessment data we collect during the learning process, not after the instructional cycle is completed. These assessments for learning, or formative assessments, are shown to have the greatest positive impact on student achievement (National Mathematics Advisory Panel 2008). Assessment for learning is an ongoing process that includes a variety of strategies and protocols to inform the progression of student learning.

One might ask, "So, what is the big difference? Don't all assessments accomplish the same goal?" The answer to those key questions is *no*. A great difference is the fact that formative assessment is designed to make student thinking visible. This is a real transformation for many teachers because when the emphasis is on student thinking and reasoning, the focus shifts from whether the answer is correct or incorrect to how the students grapple with a problem. Making student thinking visible entails a change in the manner in which teachers interact with their students. For instance, instead of relying solely on students' written work, teachers gather information through observation, questioning, and listening to their students discuss strategies, justify their reasoning, and explain why they chose to make particular decisions or use a specific representation. Since observations happen in real time, teachers can react in the moment by making an appropriate instructional decision, which may mean asking a well-posed question or suggesting a different model to represent the problem at hand.

Students are often asked to explain what they were thinking as they completed a procedure. Their response is often a recitation of the steps that were used. Such an explanation does not shed any light on whether a student understands the procedure, why it works, or if it will always work. Nor does it provide teachers with any insight into whether a student has a superficial or a deep understanding of the mathematics involved. If, however, students are encouraged to explain their thought processes, teachers will be able to discern the level of understanding. The vocabulary students use (or do not use) and the confidence with which they are able to answer probing questions can also provide insight into their levels of comprehension.

Management and Assessment (cont.)

Assessment for Learning (cont.)

One of the most important features of formative assessment is that it actively involves students in their own learning. In assessment for learning, students are asked to reflect on their own work. They may be asked to consider multiple representations of a problem and then decide which of those representations makes the most sense, or which is the most efficient, or how they relate to one another. Students may be asked to make conjectures and then prove or disprove them by negation or counterexamples. Notice that it is the students doing the hard work of making decisions and thinking through the mathematical processes. Students who work at this level of mathematics, regardless of their grade level, demonstrate a deep understanding of mathematical concepts.

Assessment for learning makes learning a shared endeavor between teachers and students. In effective learning environments students take responsibility for their learning and feel safe taking risks, and teachers have opportunities to gain a deeper understanding of what their students know and are able to do. Implementing a variety of tools and protocols when assessing for learning can help the process become seamless. Some specific formative assessment tools and protocols include:

- Student Response Forms or Journals
- Range Questions
- Gallery Walks
- Observation Protocols
- Feedback
- Exit Cards

Student Response Forms or Journals

Providing students with an organized workspace for the problems they solve can help a teacher to better understand a student's thinking and more easily identify misconceptions. Students often think that recording an answer is enough. If students do include further details, they often only write enough to fill the limited space that might be provided on an activity sheet. To promote the expectation that students show all of their work and record more of their thinking, use the included *Student Response Form* (page 130; studentresponse.pdf), or have students use a designated journal or notebook for solving problems. The prompts on the *Student Response Form* and the additional space provided encourage students to offer more details.

Range Questions

Range questions allow for a variety of responses, and teachers can use them to quickly gain access to students' understanding. Range questions are included in the activate section of many mini-lessons. The questions or problems that are posed are designed to provide insight into the spectrum of understanding that your students bring to the day's problems. For instance, you might ask *What can you tell me about these coins?* One student might note that there are 12 coins, while another might say that there are two more nickels than quarters. Yet another student might declare that the total value of the coins is $1.03. The level of sophistication in the responses varies and can help you decide which students to assign to which of the leveled problems.

Management and Assessment *(cont.)*

Gallery Walks

Gallery walks can be used in many ways, but they all promote the sharing of students' problem-solving strategies and solutions. Pairs or small groups of students can record their pictures, tables, graphs, diagrams, computational procedures, and justifications on chart paper that they hang in designated areas of the classroom prior to the debriefing component of the lesson. Or, simply have students place their *Student Response Forms* at their workspaces and have students take a tour of their classmates' thinking. Though suggested occasionally for specific mini-lessons, you can include this strategy with any of the mini-lessons.

Observation Protocols

Observation protocols facilitate the data gathering that teachers must do as they document evidence of student learning. Assessment of learning is a key component in a teacher's ability to say, "I know that my students can apply these mathematical ideas because I have this evidence." Some important learning behaviors for teachers to focus on include: level of engagement in the problem/task; incorporation of multiple representations; inclusion of appropriate labels in pictures, tables, graphs, and solutions; use of accountable talk; inclusion of reflection on their work; and connections made between and among other mathematical ideas, previous problems, and their own life experiences. There is no one right form, nor could all of these areas be included on a form while leaving room for comments. Protocols should be flexible and allow teachers to identify categories of learning important to them and their students. Two observation forms are provided in the appendices—one can be used with individual students (page 131; individualobs.pdf), and one can be used when observing a group (page 132; groupobs.pdf).

Feedback

Feedback is a critical component of formative assessment. Teachers who do not give letter grades on projects, quizzes, or tests, but who provide either neutral feedback or inquisitive feedback, find their students take a greater interest in the work they receive back than they did when their papers were graded. There are different types of feedback, but effective feedback focuses on the evidence in student work. Many students respond favorably to an "assessment sandwich." The first comment might be a positive comment or praise for something well done, followed by a critical question or request for further clarification, followed by another neutral or positive comment.

Exit Cards

Exit cards are an effective way of assessing students' thinking at the end of a lesson in preparation for future instruction. There are multiple ways in which exit cards can be used. A similar problem to the one students have previously solved can be posed, or students can be asked to identify topics of confusion, what they liked best, or what they think they learned from a lesson. One simple exit card task involves distributing cards that show three thumbs: one pointing up, one pointing horizontally, and one pointing down (exitcard.pdf). Students readily pick the one that they think best reflects their understanding of the lesson and place the cards into a receptacle. As one student said as she dropped her card in the box, "This has been a great thumbs-up problem-solving day!" Exit-card tasks are suggested in the *Differentiate* sections of some of the mini-lessons, but they may be added to any mini-lesson.

How to Use This Book

Mini-Lesson Plan

Lessons are organized by **Common Core State Standards** domains.

Suggested **Problem-Solving Strategies** outline strategies students may want to use in solving the problem. However, these are not the only strategies that can be used to solve the problem.

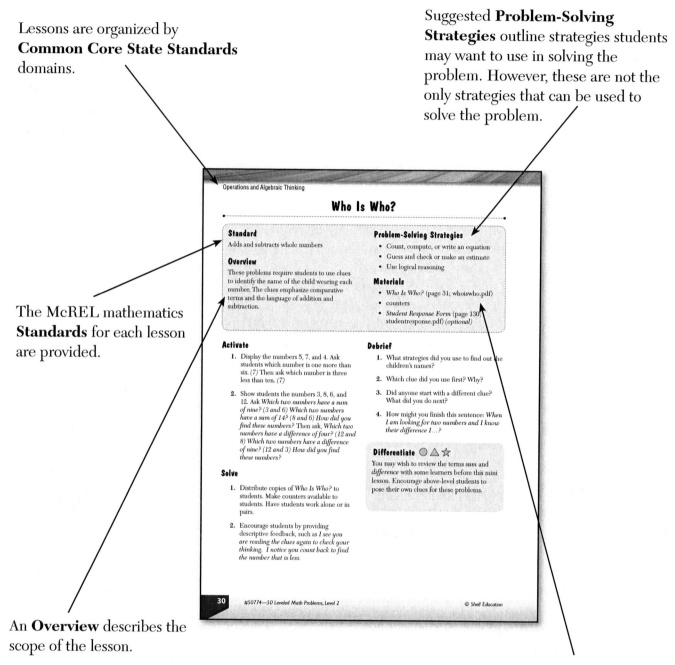

Operations and Algebraic Thinking

Who Is Who?

Standard

Adds and subtracts whole numbers

Overview

These problems require students to use clues to identify the name of the child wearing each number. The clues emphasize comparative terms and the language of addition and subtraction.

Problem-Solving Strategies

- Count, compute, or write an equation
- Guess and check or make an estimate
- Use logical reasoning

Materials

- *Who Is Who?* (page 31; whoiswho.pdf)
- counters
- *Student Response Form* (page 130; studentresponse.pdf) *(optional)*

Activate

1. Display the numbers 5, 7, and 4. Ask students which number is one more than six. (7) Then ask which number is three less than ten. (7)

2. Show students the numbers 3, 8, 6, and 12. Ask *Which two numbers have a sum of nine?* (3 and 6) *Which two numbers have a sum of 14?* (8 and 6) *How did you find these numbers?* Then ask, *Which two numbers have a difference of four?* (12 and 8) *Which two numbers have a difference of nine?* (12 and 3) *How did you find these numbers?*

Solve

1. Distribute copies of *Who Is Who?* to students. Make counters available to students. Have students work alone or in pairs.

2. Encourage students by providing descriptive feedback, such as *I see you are reading the clues again to check your thinking. I notice you count back to find the number that is less.*

Debrief

1. What strategies did you use to find out the children's names?

2. Which clue did you use first? Why?

3. Did anyone start with a different clue? What did you do next?

4. How might you finish this sentence: *When I am looking for two numbers and I know their difference I…?*

Differentiate ◯ △ ☆

You may wish to review the terms *sum* and *difference* with some learners before this mini lesson. Encourage above-level students to pose their own clues for these problems.

30 #50774—50 Leveled Math Problems, Level 2   © Shell Education

The McREL mathematics **Standards** for each lesson are provided.

An **Overview** describes the scope of the lesson.

The **Materials** section lists the items needed for each lesson.

How to Use This Book *(cont.)*

Mini-Lesson Plan *(cont.)*

The **Activate** section suggests how you can access or assess students' prior knowledge. This section might recommend ways to have students review vocabulary, recall experiences related to the problem contexts, remember relevant mathematical ideas, or solve simpler related problems.

The **Solve** section provides suggestions on how to group students for the problem they will solve. It also provides questions to ask, observations to make, or procedures to follow to guide students in their work.

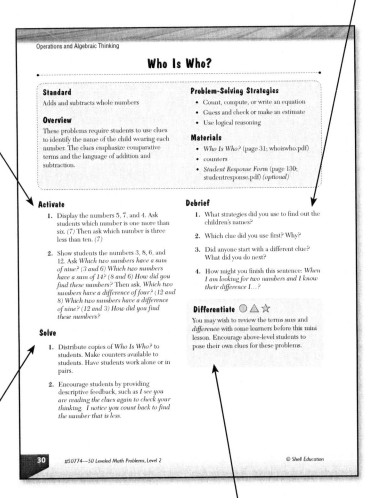

Operations and Algebraic Thinking

Who Is Who?

Standard
Adds and subtracts whole numbers

Overview
These problems require students to use clues to identify the name of the child wearing each number. The clues emphasize comparative terms and the language of addition and subtraction.

Problem-Solving Strategies
• Count, compute, or write an equation
• Guess and check or make an estimate
• Use logical reasoning

Materials
• *Who Is Who?* (page 31; whoiswho.pdf)
• counters
• *Student Response Form* (page 130; studentresponse.pdf) *(optional)*

Activate
1. Display the numbers 5, 7, and 4. Ask students which number is one more than six. (7) Then ask which number is three less than ten. (7)
2. Show students the numbers 3, 8, 6, and 12. Ask *Which two numbers have a sum of nine?* (3 and 6) *Which two numbers have a sum of 14?* (8 and 6) *How did you find these numbers?* Then ask, *Which two numbers have a difference of four?* (12 and 8) *Which two numbers have a difference of nine?* (12 and 3) *How did you find these numbers?*

Solve
1. Distribute copies of *Who Is Who?* to students. Make counters available to students. Have students work alone or in pairs.
2. Encourage students by providing descriptive feedback, such as *I see you are reading the clues again to check your thinking. I notice you count back to find the number that is less.*

Debrief
1. What strategies did you use to find out the children's names?
2. Which clue did you use first? Why?
3. Did anyone start with a different clue? What did you do next?
4. How might you finish this sentence: *When I am looking for two numbers and I know their difference I…?*

Differentiate ○ △ ☆
You may wish to review the terms *sum* and *difference* with some learners before this mini lesson. Encourage above-level students to pose their own clues for these problems.

30   #50774—50 Leveled Math Problems, Level 2   © Shell Education

The **Debrief** section provides questions designed to deepen students' understanding of the mathematics and the problem-solving process. Because the leveled problems share common features, it is possible to debrief either with small groups or as a whole class.

The **Differentiate** section includes additional suggestions to meet the unique needs of students. This section may offer support for English language learners, scaffolding for below-level students, or enrichment opportunities for above-level students. The following symbols are used to indicate appropriate readiness levels for the differentiation:

○   below level

▢   on level

△   above level

☆   English language learner

How to Use This Book *(cont.)*

Lesson Resources

Leveled Problems

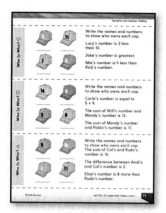

Each activity sheet offers **leveled problems** at three levels of challenge—below-level, on-level, and above-level. Cut the activity sheet apart and distribute the appropriate problem to each student, or present all of the leveled problems on an activity sheet to every student.

Record-Keeping Chart

Use the **Record-Keeping Chart** (page 133) to keep track of the problems each student completes.

Observation Forms

Use the **Individual Observation Form** (page 131) to document students' progress as they work through problems on their own. Use the **Group Observation Form** (page 132) to keep a record of students' success in working with their peers to solve problems.

Teacher Resource CD

Helpful reproducibles are provided on the accompanying **Teacher Resource CD**. A detailed listing of the CD contents can be found on pages 140–141. The CD includes:

- Resources to support the implementation of the mini-lessons
- Manipulative templates
- Reproducible PDFs of all leveled problems and assessment tools
- Correlations to standards

How to Use This Book (cont.)

Lesson Resources (cont.)

Student Response Form

Students can attach their leveled problem to the form.

Students have space to show their work, provide their solution, and explain their thinking.

Appendix A

Name: _____ Date: _____

Student Response Form

Problem:

(glue your problem here)

My Work and Illustrations: *(picture, table, list, graph)*   **My Solution:**

My Explanation:

_____

_____

130   #50774—50 Leveled Math Problems, Level 2   © Shell Education

Correlations to Standards

Shell Education is committed to producing educational materials that are research- and standards-based. In this effort, we have correlated all of our products to the academic standards of all 50 United States, the District of Columbia, the Department of Defense Dependent Schools, and all Canadian provinces. We have also correlated to the Common Core State Standards.

How To Find Standards Correlations

To print a customized correlation report of this product for your state, visit our website at **http://www.shelleducation.com** and follow the on-screen directions. If you require assistance in printing correlation reports, please contact Customer Service at 1-877-777-3450.

Purpose and Intent of Standards

Legislation mandates that all states adopt academic standards that identify the skills students will learn in kindergarten through grade twelve. Many states also have standards for Pre-K. This same legislation sets requirements to ensure the standards are detailed and comprehensive.

Standards are designed to focus instruction and guide adoption of curricula. Standards are statements that describe the criteria necessary for students to meet specific academic goals. They define the knowledge, skills, and content students should acquire at each level. Standards are also used to develop standardized tests to evaluate students' academic progress. Teachers are required to demonstrate how their lessons meet state standards. State standards are used in the development of all of our products, so educators can be assured they meet the academic requirements of each state.

McREL Compendium

We use the Mid-continent Research for Education and Learning (McREL) Compendium to create standards correlations. Each year, McREL analyzes state standards and revises the compendium. By following this procedure, McREL is able to produce a general compilation of national standards. Each lesson in this product is based on one or more McREL standards, which are listed on the Teacher Resource CD (mcrel.pdf).

TESOL Standards

The lessons in this book promote English language development for English language learners. The standards listed on the Teacher Resource CD (tesol.pdf) support the language objectives presented throughout the lessons.

Common Core State Standards

The lessons in this book are aligned to the Common Core State Standards (CCSS). The standards listed on pages 27–29 (ccss.pdf) support the objectives presented throughout the lessons.

NCTM Standards

The lessons in this book are aligned to the National Council of Teachers of Mathematics (NCTM) standards. The standards listed on the Teacher Resource CD (nctm.pdf) support the objectives presented throughout the lessons.

Correlations to Standards (cont.)

Common Core State Standards Correlation

Common Core Standard	Lesson
2.OA.1 Use addition and subtraction within 100 to solve one- and two-step word problems involving situations of adding to, taking from, putting together, taking apart, and comparing, with unknowns in all positions, e.g., by using drawings and equations with a symbol for the unknown number to represent the problem.	Who Is Who?, page 30; Design Blocks, page 32; Yard Sale, page 34; Books for Sale, page 40; Field Day, page 46; Bagfuls, page 50; Salad Garden, page 52; What Am I Thinking?, page 54; Puzzlers, page 58; Animal Stories, page 60; Lots of Ribbon, page 94; Money Matters, page 112
2.OA.2 Fluently add and subtract within 20 using mental strategies. By end of Grade 2, know from memory all sums of two one-digit numbers.	Who Is Who?, page 30; Design Blocks, page 32; Yard Sale, page 34; Equal Sums, page 36; Books for Sale, page 40; Make a Face, page 44; Bagfuls, page 50; Salad Garden, page 52; What Am I Thinking?, page 54; Animal Stories, page 60
2.OA.3 Determine whether a group of objects (up to 20) has an odd or even number of members, e.g., by pairing objects or counting them by 2s; write an equation to express an even number as a sum of two equal addends.	Venn Diagrams, page 38
2.OA.4 Use addition to find the total number of objects arranged in rectangular arrays with up to 5 rows and up to 5 columns; write an equation to express the total as a sum of equal addends.	Salad Garden, page 52
2.NBT.1 Understand that the three digits of a three-digit number represent amounts of hundreds, tens, and ones; e.g., 706 equals 7 hundreds, 0 tens, and 6 ones. Understand the following as special cases: 100 can be thought of as a bundle of ten tens — called a "hundred." The numbers 100, 200, 300, 400, 500, 600, 700, 800, 900 refer to one, two, three, four, five, six, seven, eight, or nine hundreds (and 0 tens and 0 ones).	Living on Main Street, page 68; Show It, page 72; Ring Toss, page 78
2.NBT.2 Count within 1,000; skip-count by 5s, 10s, and 100s.	Predict the Number, page 66; Where Is It?, page 74; Ring Toss, page 78; Counting Along, page 80; All About Us, page 86; Last Names, page 88
2.NBT.3 Read and write numbers to 1,000 using base-ten numerals, number names, and expanded form.	Number Blocks, page 62; Living on Main Street, page 68; Show It, page 72; Ring Toss, page 78

The left side of the table has a vertical label for the first four rows: **Operations and Algebraic Thinking**, and for the last three rows: **Number and Operations in Base Ten**.

Correlations to Standards (cont.)

Common Core State Standards Correlation (cont.)

	Common Core Standard	Lesson
Number and Operations in Base Ten (cont.)	**2.NBT.5** Fluently add and subtract within 100 using strategies based on place value, properties of operations, and/or the relationship between addition and subtraction.	Make a Face, page 44; Field Day, page 46; Pose a Problem, page 48; What Am I Thinking?, page 54; Same Sums, page 56; Puzzlers, page 58; Animal Stories, page 60; Figure It, page 64; Machine Math, page 70; Where Is It?, page 74; Finish the Equations, page 76; From the Beginning, page 84; Lots of Ribbon, page 94
	2.NBT.7 Add and subtract within 1,000, using concrete models or drawings and strategies based on place value, properties of operations, and/or the relationship between addition and subtraction; relate the strategy to a written method. Understand that in adding or subtracting three-digit numbers, one adds or subtracts hundreds and hundreds, tens and tens, ones and ones; and sometimes it is necessary to compose or decompose tens or hundreds.	Number Blocks, page 62; Where Is It?, page 74; Ring Toss, page 78
	2.NBT.8 Mentally add 10 or 100 to a given number 100–900, and mentally subtract 10 or 100 from a given number 100–900.	Where Is It?, page 74
	2.NBT.9 Explain why addition and subtraction strategies work, using place value and the properties of operations.	Puzzlers, page 58
Measurement and Data	**2.MD.1** Measure the length of an object by selecting and using appropriate tools such as rulers, yardsticks, meter sticks, and measuring tapes.	Measure It, page 90; Find the Lengths, page 92; Finish the Story, page 96
	2.MD.2 Measure the length of an object twice, using length units of different lengths for the two measurements; describe how the two measurements relate to the size of the unit chosen.	Step-by-Step, page 98
	2.MD.5 Use addition and subtraction within 100 to solve word problems involving lengths that are given in the same units, e.g., by using drawings (such as drawings of rulers) and equations with a symbol for the unknown number to represent the problem.	Lots of Ribbon, page 94
	2.MD.6 Represent whole numbers as lengths from 0 on a number line diagram with equally spaced points corresponding to the numbers 0, 1, 2, …, and represent whole-number sums and differences within 100 on a number line diagram.	Where Is It?, page 74

Correlations to Standards (cont.)

Common Core State Standards Correlation (cont.)

Common Core Standard	Lesson
2.MD.7 Tell and write time from analog and digital clocks to the nearest five minutes, using A.M. and P.M.	Game Time, page 100; Tell a Story, page 102; Leo's Days, page 104
2.MD.8 Solve word problems involving dollar bills, quarters, dimes, nickels, and pennies, using $ and ¢ symbols appropriately. Example: If you have 2 dimes and 3 pennies, how many cents do you have?	Coin Combos, page 106; Joke Sale, page 108; All My Coins, page 110; Money Matters, page 112
2.MD.9 Generate measurement data by measuring lengths of several objects to the nearest whole unit, or by making repeated measurements of the same object. Show the measurements by making a line plot, where the horizontal scale is marked off in whole-number units.	Measure It, page 90; Step-by-Step, page 98
2.MD.10 Draw a picture graph and a bar graph (with single-unit scale) to represent a data set with up to four categories. Solve simple put-together, take-apart, and compare problems using information presented in a bar graph.	All About Us, page 86; All My Coins, page 110
2.G.1 Recognize and draw shapes having specified attributes, such as a given number of angles or a given number of equal faces. Identify triangles, quadrilaterals, pentagons, hexagons, and cubes.	What Shape Is Next?, page 114; What Shape Am I?, page 116; Shape Symbols, page 122; How Many Cubes?, page 124; Find the Triangles, page 128
2.G.2 Partition a rectangle into rows and columns of same-size squares and count to find the total number of them.	Dot Squares, page 120
2.G.3 Partition circles and rectangles into two, three, or four equal shares, describe the shares using the words halves, thirds, half of, a third of, etc., and describe the whole as two halves, three thirds, four fourths. Recognize that equal shares of identical wholes need not have the same shape.	Make the Whole, page 126

The rows from 2.MD.7 through 2.MD.10 are labeled along the left side: **Measurement and Data (cont.)**. The rows 2.G.1 through 2.G.3 are labeled along the left side: **Geometry**.

Who Is Who?

Standard

Adds and subtracts whole numbers

Overview

These problems require students to use clues to identify the name of the child wearing each number. The clues emphasize comparative terms and the language of addition and subtraction.

Problem-Solving Strategies

- Count, compute, or write an equation
- Guess and check or make an estimate
- Use logical reasoning

Materials

- *Who Is Who?* (page 31; whoiswho.pdf)
- counters
- *Student Response Form* (page 130; studentresponse.pdf) *(optional)*

Activate

1. Display the numbers 5, 7, and 4. Ask students which number is one more than six. *(7)* Then ask which number is three less than ten. *(7)*

2. Show students the numbers 3, 8, 6, and 12. Ask *Which two numbers have a sum of nine? (3 and 6) Which two numbers have a sum of 14? (8 and 6) How did you find these numbers?* Then, ask *Which two numbers have a difference of four? (12 and 8) Which two numbers have a difference of nine? (12 and 3) How did you find these numbers?*

Solve

1. Distribute copies of *Who Is Who?* to students. Make counters available to students. Have students work alone or in pairs.

2. Encourage students by providing descriptive feedback, such as *I see you are reading the clues again to check your thinking. I notice you count back to find the number that is less.*

Debrief

1. What strategies did you use to find the children's numbers?

2. Which clue did you use first? Why?

3. Did anyone start with a different clue? What did you do next?

4. How might you finish this sentence: *When I am looking for two numbers and I know their difference is 1…?*

Differentiate ◯ △ ☆

You may wish to review the terms *sum* and *difference* with some learners before this mini-lesson. Encourage above-level students to pose their own clues for these problems.

Write the names to show who owns each cap.

Lucy's number is 3 less than 10.

Jake's number is greatest.

Mia's number is 4 less than Rick's number.

 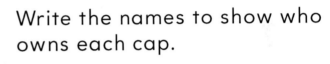

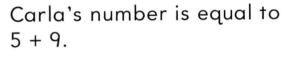

Write the names to show who owns each cap.

Carla's number is equal to 5 + 9.

The sum of Will's number and Mandy's number is 12.

The sum of Mandy's number and Pablo's number is 11.

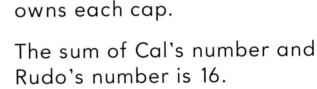

Write the names to show who owns each cap.

The sum of Cal's number and Rudo's number is 16.

The difference between Andi's number and Cal's number is 2.

Eliza's number is 8 more than Rudo's number.

Design Blocks

Standards

- Solves real-world problems involving addition and subtraction of whole numbers
- Uses the names of simple geometric shapes to represent and describe real-world situations

Overview

These problems require students to compare the number of shapes children use in each of their designs. Students interpret comparative language and in the last two problems, meet multiple problem conditions.

Problem-Solving Strategies

- Act it out or use manipulatives
- Organize information in a picture, list, table, graph, or diagram

Materials

- *Design Blocks* (page 33; designblocks.pdf)
- pattern blocks
- counters *(optional)*
- *Student Response Form* (page 130; studentresponse.pdf) *(optional)*

Activate

1. Distribute pattern blocks to students and allow a few minutes for them to build individual designs. Ask students questions about the designs they built, for example *Who used more than three hexagons in their design? Who used less than five triangles? Who used exactly five squares?*

2. Observe students' designs to gather data for a problem such as *I see Sara used four triangles in her design and Nathan used five more triangles than Sara did. How many triangles did Nathan use?* Record the expression *4 + 5* on the board. Then, ask students how many triangles they used in all. Record the equation *4 + 9 = 13.*

Solve

1. Distribute copies of *Design Blocks* to students. Have students work alone, in pairs, or in small groups.

2. Note the representations students use as they work to find solutions.

Debrief

1. What strategies could you use to solve the problem?

2. What equation could you write to find the answer?

3. How could a list help you solve the problem?

Differentiate ⬤ ⬛ ☆

Some students may be distracted by the colors and shapes of the pattern blocks but still need to use manipulatives. Have them work at a table with counters once they begin to focus on the problems.

Design Blocks

Matt has 13 squares.

He uses 7 of the squares in his design.

How many squares does Matt have left to use?

Design Blocks

Tia and Nadia each build a design.

Together they use 12 triangles.

Tia has more than 4 triangles in her design.

What is the greatest number of triangles Nadia could have?

Design Blocks

James and Henry each build a design.

Together they use 15 hexagons.

James has fewer than 8 hexagons in his design.

How many hexagons could each child have?

Yard Sale

Standards

- Adds and subtracts whole numbers
- Solves real-world problems involving addition and subtraction of whole numbers

Overview

Students are shown objects for sale at a yard sale and determine the total amount spent by a customer or the value of one of the items someone bought.

Problem-Solving Strategies

- Count, compute, or write an equation
- Use logical reasoning

Materials

- *Yard Sale* (page 35; yardsale.pdf)
- *Student Response Form* (page 130; studentresponse.pdf) *(optional)*

Activate

1. Ask students if they have ever had or been to a yard sale (or tag sale or garage sale, depending on the term used in your region). Have a few students respond.

2. Have a student identify an item that might be bought at a yard sale. Write the name of the item on the board and give it a price of $5.00. Have another student name a different item and again record it on the board, along with a price of $7.00.

3. Have students talk with a neighbor about the math questions they could ask and answer with this information.

4. Encourage several pairs of students to give examples of questions. For each question, have another pair of students write the related equation, and still another pair find the answer.

Solve

1. Distribute copies of *Yard Sale* to students. Have students work individually, in pairs, or in small groups.

2. If students are working with others, observe how they interact. Does each student contribute to the solution? Do they build on one another's ideas?

Debrief

1. How did you find your answer?

2. Is there a different way to solve the problem?

3. What equation could we write for this problem?

Differentiate ○ ■

Open number lines can help students keep track of their thinking. If a student makes an open number line, ask clarifying questions to make the students' thinking more explicit. For example, *What number are you showing now? How are you splitting up this number?*

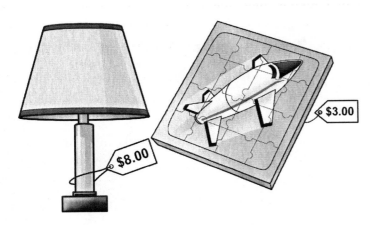

Carlos buys a lamp and a puzzle. How much does Carlos spend?

Write an equation to solve this problem.

Lucy buys these two items at the sale. She spends $14.00. How much does the teddy bear cost?

Write an equation to solve this problem.

Riley buys two baseballs and one soccer ball. She spends $15.00. Each baseball costs the same amount. How much does one baseball cost?

Write an equation to solve this problem.

Equal Sums

Standard

Adds and subtracts whole numbers

Overview

Students are presented with four sets of numbers. Their task is to move one number from one set to another so that each set of numbers has the same sum.

Problem-Solving Strategies

- Count, compute, or write an equation
- Find information in a picture, list, table, graph, or diagram
- Guess and check or make an estimate
- Use logical reasoning

Materials

- *Equal Sums* (page 37; equalsums.pdf)
- *Number Cards* (numbercards.pdf)
- *Student Response Form* (page 130; studentresponse.pdf) *(optional)*

Activate

1. Display the numbers 5, 7, 3, and 1. Have students use these numbers to write two addition equations with equal sums. *(5 + 3 = 8; 7 + 1 = 8)* Ask students what it means to be *equal*.

2. Have students share their responses and ask them how they were able to identify how to group the numbers. Record 5 + 3 = 7 + 1 to emphasize the equality of the sums.

3. Display the following two groups of numbers: 3, 4, 9 and 6, 1, 3. Ask *What if we wanted each of these groups to have the same sum? Do you think we should move a number from the first set or the second set? Why?* Invite students to talk to a partner about which number to move and have pairs identify their solutions and strategies. As before, record 4 + 9 = 3 + 6 + 1 + 3 to emphasize the equality of the sums.

Solve

1. Distribute copies of *Equal Sums* to students. Have students work alone or in pairs.

2. Point out to students that they will move only one number to create groups of numbers with the same sum. Make copies of *Number Cards* available to students who wish to use them.

3. Observe students as they work. How do they find the sums?

Debrief

1. What number did you move? How did you decide on that number?

2. How does finding the sum of each group help you decide what to do?

Differentiate ☐ △

Many students will find solutions through guessing and checking and moving the number cards as they do so. Some will recognize that they need to move a number from the set with the greatest sum to the set that has the least sum. Encourage these students to explain their thinking so that other students can be exposed to more abstract approaches.

Equal Sums

Box 1		
1	6	6

Box 2		
1	8	5

Box 3		
4	3	6

Box 4		
1	6	5

Move one number to another box.

The sum of the numbers in each box must be 13.

Circle the number and draw an arrow to show the move.

Equal Sums

Box 1			
6	5	4	2

Box 2		
5	7	5

Box 3		
9	8	4

Box 4		
2	4	7

Move one number to another box.

The sum of the numbers in each box must be equal.

Circle the number and draw an arrow to show the move.

Equal Sums

Box 1			
8	4	9	7

Box 2			
12	7	10	5

Box 3			
16	3	1	14

Box 4			
6	21	4	9

Move one number to another box.

The sum of the numbers in each box must be equal.

Circle the number and draw an arrow to show the move.

Venn Diagrams

Standard

Uses base-ten concepts to compare whole-number relationships

Overview

Students are shown two-ring Venn diagrams and decide where given numbers should be placed in the diagram based on the given labels, or identify possible labels when shown where given numbers are placed.

Problem-Solving Strategies

- Act it out or use manipulatives
- Find information in a picture, list, table, graph, or diagram
- Use logical reasoning

Materials

- *Venn Diagrams* (page 39; venndiagrams.pdf)
- *Number Cards* (numbercards.pdf)
- two hula hoops or two 3-ft. pieces of string or yarn, tied in a loop
- counters
- *Student Response Form* (page 130; studentresponse.pdf) *(optional)*

Activate

1. Place the two hoops or yarn loops in an open area or on a large table. Overlap the hoops to create a Venn diagram. Write *even* on one piece of paper and *less than 3* on the other. Place one of these labels just above each of the rings.

2. From *Number Cards*, randomly choose a card 1–6 and ask, *Is this number even? How do you know? Is this number less than 3? How do you know? Where should we put this number in the diagram to show this?* Place the card in the appropriate place.

3. Have a student take a card and decide where it should be placed in the diagram. Ask the student why he or she placed the number in that particular spot. Ask the class if anyone disagrees, and if so, to explain their thinking.

4. Repeat this activity until all of the cards are placed correctly.

Solve

1. Distribute copies of *Venn Diagrams* to students. Have students work alone, in pairs, or in small groups.

2. Observe how the students decide where the numbers should be placed. Do they consider each number individually, deciding how it compares to the two labels? Do they prefer to consider one region at a time, writing all of the numbers that fit those criteria?

Debrief

1. How did you decide where to put the numbers?

2. Where might other numbers go in these regions?

Differentiate

Students may want to use counters to check if a number is even or odd by attempting to create evenly-split groups.

Complete the diagram using the numbers 1–8.

Even Numbers   Greater than 6

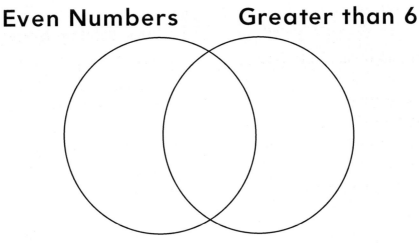

Complete the diagram using the numbers 7–14.

Less than 11   Odd Numbers

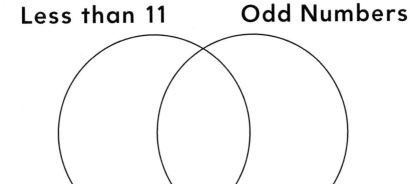

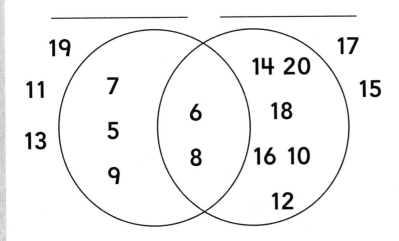

Josie placed the numbers 5–20 in the diagram.

Look at how she sorted the numbers and decide what the categories are.

Label the two sides of the diagram.

Books for Sale

Standard

Solves real-world problems involving addition and subtraction of whole numbers

Overview

Students identify the amount of money given to a clerk and the change received. Once students have determined the total cost, they must consider the books and prices shown and decide which ones were bought.

Problem-Solving Strategies

- Count, compute, or write an equation
- Find information in a picture, list, table, graph, or diagram
- Guess and check or make an estimate

Materials

- *Books for Sale* (page 41; booksforsale.pdf)
- play money (dollar bills) *(optional)*
- *Student Response Form* (page 130; studentresponse.pdf) *(optional)*

Activate

1. Have students brainstorm different types of books. Encourage a variety of categories to be considered. If time allows, have students identify some of their favorite books in each category.

2. Display the following problem for students: *I bought a mystery book for $5.00 and a book about snakes for $4.00. I gave the clerk $10.00. What was my change?* ($1.00)

3. Have students talk with a neighbor about the answer.

4. Have students share their answers and strategies. Then, ask them why some people might call this a two-step problem.

Solve

1. Distribute copies of *Books for Sale* to students. Have students work individually, in pairs, or in small groups.

2. Ask clarifying questions as students work to help them focus on the multiple steps of the problems. For example, ask *What did you just find? What are you doing now? What will you do next?*

Debrief

1. How did you find the answer?

2. Is there a different way to solve the problem?

3. What is another problem we could create using these books and prices?

Differentiate ◯ ☆

Make the play money available to students who wish to act out these problems. Some students find it helpful to think of two-step problems as problems with a missing question. In these problems the missing question would be: *How much did the books cost?*

The library had a book sale to make room for new books.

I bought two of these books.

I gave the clerk $10.00.

I got $3.00 back in change.

Which two books did I buy?

The library had a book sale to make room for new books.

I bought two of these books.

I gave the clerk $20.00.

I got $8.00 back in change.

Which two books did I buy?

The library had a book sale to make room for new books.

I bought three of these books.

I gave the clerk $20.00.

I got $2.00 back in change.

Which three books did I buy?

Books for Sale

Books for Sale

Books for Sale

Rubber Band Shapes

Standard

Adds and subtracts whole numbers

Overview

This problem set focuses on students posing questions. The data given suggests questions related to sums, differences, and comparisons

Problem-Solving Strategies

- Guess and check or make an estimate
- Work backward

Materials

- *Rubber Band Shapes* (page 43; rubberband.pdf)
- sticky notes *(optional)*
- *Student Response Form* (page 130; studentresponse.pdf) *(optional)*

Activate

1. Announce to students that the answer to a question is 7 and it is their job to figure out the question. Encourage students to provide multiple responses, such as *What is the number between 6 and 8? How many days are there in a week? What is 12 – 5?* Repeat the activity for the number 25.

2. Display the following information for students: *Salim has 35 rubber band shapes. Jodie has 22 rubber band shapes.* Tell students the answer to a question about these bands is 13. Ask them what the question could be. Have students talk with a partner to identify a question, then have partners share their ideas with the class. If all the students suggest *How many more bands does Salim have than Jodie?*, ask if anyone can think of a question with the word *fewer* in it.

3. Repeat the activity in step 2 using the same information, but tell students that the answer to a new question is 57.

Solve

1. Distribute copies of *Rubber Band Shapes* to students. Have students work alone, in pairs, or in small groups.

2. Provide encouraging feedback, such as *I see you tried many possibilities to find the answer. I notice you are using correct math vocabulary.*

3. Ask refocusing questions, such as *How might knowing the answer help you?*

Debrief

1. What question did you find?

2. Did anyone ask a different question for that answer?

3. What helped you to think of questions?

4. What other answer could there be? What question could we ask for this answer?

Differentiate ○ ◻

Some students will find it easier to identify questions if they write the numbers down on sticky notes. Students can then combine the numbers in different ways and check to see if their sum or difference matches an answer.

Use the information below. Talk with a partner. Write a question for each answer.

Emily has 15 animal bands.

Nigel has 8 animal bands and 10 people bands.

Answers: 23   7

Use the information below. Talk with a partner. Write a question for each answer.

Wendell has 10 animal bands and 17 people bands.

Pablo has 26 animal bands.

Answers: 36   16   7

Use the information below. Talk with a partner. Write a question for each answer.

Li Ming has 44 animal bands and 16 people bands.

Tala has 18 animal bands and 48 people bands.

Answers: 60   30   26   6

Make a Face

Standard

Solves real-world problems involving addition and subtraction of whole numbers

Overview

Students are shown a variety of parts of faces (eyes, nose, mouth, etc.) and corresponding point values. Students either find total values for faces shown or draw a face for given total values.

Problem-Solving Strategies

- Count, compute, or write an equation
- Find information in a picture, list, table, graph, or diagram
- Guess and check or make an estimate

Materials

- *Make a Face* (page 45; makeface.pdf)
- *Student Response Form* (page 130; studentresponse.pdf) *(optional)*

Activate

1. Ask students if they have ever made an avatar, worn a disguise, or played with Mr. Potato Head™. Have students describe these activities for those who may be unfamiliar with them. Ask students what these activities have in common.

2. Have students find $8 + 6 + 2$ and share their strategies for doing so. Record their ideas for all to see.

Solve

1. Distribute copies of *Make a Face* to students. Have students work alone, in pairs, or in small groups.

2. As students work, ask questions such as *How did you add (or subtract) these numbers? Why?*

3. Before debriefing, have students take a gallery walk to see how others recorded their thinking or to see the faces that were drawn. As students take this walk, listen to their comments to learn what they notice and what connections they make.

Debrief

1. How did you find the answer?

2. Did anyone use a different strategy?

3. Can we find the difference between the number of points Jia Li and Brad used without adding all of the points for each face? (Note: As both faces have noses, it could be eliminated from each sum.)

4. What did you notice on your gallery walk?

Differentiation ◐ ■ △ ☆

Some partners may enjoy creating faces and exchanging them with one another to determine the total points.

6 points	5 points	2 points	12 points
4 points	10 points	8 points	6 points

How many points do you need to make this face?

6 points	5 points	2 points	12 points
4 points	10 points	8 points	6 points

How many more points did Brad use than Jia Li?

Jia Li   **Brad**

 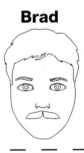

6 points	5 points	2 points	12 points
4 points	10 points	8 points	6 points

Make two faces. One should have 11 more points than the other.

Field Day

Standard

Solves real-world problems involving addition and subtraction of whole numbers

Overview

These problems require students to work backward to find the number of children that entered a particular event at a field day.

Problem-Solving Strategies

- Count, compute, or write an equation
- Organize information in a picture, list, table, graph, or diagram
- Work backward

Materials

- *Field Day* (page 47; fieldday.pdf)
- *Student Response Form* (page 130; studentresponse.pdf) *(optional)*

Activate

1. Ask students what activities there might be at a school field day. Allow several students to respond.

2. Display the following problem for students: *There were 12 more second graders at Field Day than third graders. There were 52 third graders at Field Day. How many second graders were at Field Day? (64)* Have students work in pairs to find the answer. Have the pairs share their strategies. If no one suggests the use of a number line, show how this might be used. You may want to challenge some students to use only mental computation.

Solve

1. Distribute copies of *Field Day* to students. Have students work alone, in pairs, or in small groups.

2. Ask clarifying and refocusing questions as students work, such as *How did you get this number? What are you trying to do now?*

3. Provide encouraging feedback, such as *I see how you found the number of children here. Your work is labeled clearly.*

Debrief

1. What answer did you find? How did you find it?

2. What fact did you have to find first?

3. What other problems have you solved like these?

Differentiation ○ ☆

Most story problems are written in a common style; the information is given in the order it is needed. In these problems, the information you need to use first is given last. To help students who are confused by this order, you may want to draw an arrow that starts beside the last piece of data and points up.

Field Day

Suzi earned 45 more points than Natasha.

Natasha earned 20 points.

How many points did Suzi earn?

Field Day

There were 12 more children in the jumping contest than in the water balloon contest.

There were 20 more children in the water balloon contest than in the softball games.

There were 36 children in the softball games.

How many children were in the water balloon contest?

How many children were in the jumping contest?

Field Day

Thirty-five more children were in the tug-of-war than the relay race.

Forty more children were in the relay race than the three-legged race.

There were 25 children in the three-legged race.

How many children were in the tug-of-war?

Pose a Problem

Standards

- Understands symbolic, concrete, and pictorial representations of numbers
- Adds and subtracts whole numbers

Overview

This problem set focuses on making connections among multiple representations. Students are shown a diagram and asked to write an equation to fit the diagram, to write a story problem to match the equation, and to solve the problem they create.

Problem-Solving Strategies

- Count, compute, or write an equation
- Find information in a picture, list, table, graph, or diagram

Materials

- *Pose a Problem* (page 49; poseaproblem.pdf)
- *Student Response Form* (page 130; studentresponse.pdf) *(optional)*

Activate

1. Display the following problem for students: *There were 72 cupcakes to sell at the second-grade bake sale. There were 31 cupcakes already sold. How many cupcakes can still be sold?* Ask students what drawing or diagram they might make to represent this story problem.

2. Encourage several responses, inviting students to share different representations. If no one suggests a bar-like model, add the following diagram to the others.

72	
31	?

Solve

1. Distribute copies of *Pose a Problem* to students. Have students work alone, in pairs, or in small groups.

2. As students work, note those who stay with the theme of a bake sale and those who introduce their own themes.

Debrief

1. How did you decide what equation to write?

2. What story problem did you create?

3. What is similar about this problem and the cupcake problem?

Differentiate ◯ ☆

You may want to meet with a small group of students to brainstorm some ideas before they create their own stories. Brainstorming a list of related words such as *treasures, pirates, maps,* and *ship* can help some students think of a problem they want to write. Some students may be able to think of a problem more easily if they replace the numbers with appropriate smaller ones.

Pose a Problem

25	5
?	

Maxi made this diagram while solving a problem.

Write an equation to fit Maxi's diagram.

Write a story problem to match the equation.

Give the answer to your problem.

Pose a Problem

32	?
53	

Tedra made this diagram while solving a problem.

Write an equation to fit Tedra's diagram.

Write a story problem to match the equation.

Give the answer to your problem.

Pose a Problem

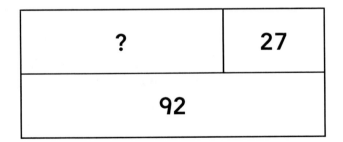

?	27
92	

Kristina made this diagram while solving a problem.

Write an equation to fit Kristina's diagram.

Write a story problem to match the equation.

Give the answer to your problem.

Bagfuls

Standards

- Counts whole numbers
- Solves real-world problems involving addition and subtraction of whole numbers

Overview

In these multistep problems students are told about equal groups of cookies, fruits, or muffins in one bag. They then determine the total number in several bags.

Problem-Solving Strategies

- Count, compute, or write an equation
- Organize information in a picture, list, table, graph, or diagram
- Use logical reasoning

Materials

- *Bagfuls* (page 51; bagfuls.pdf)
- 3 small opaque bags
- color tiles or cubes (6 total, 3 red and 3 blue)
- *Student Response Form* (page 130; studentresponse.pdf) *(optional)*

Activate

1. Gather children around the three bags. Have them watch as you place one red tile (or cube) in each bag. Then, place one blue tile (or cube) in each bag. Ask students to talk with a partner about the total number of tiles (or cubes) in these bags. Encourage students to find more than one way to decide.

2. Have the pairs report their thinking.

3. Empty the bags and count to confirm the answer.

Solve

1. Distribute copies of *Bagfuls* to students. Have students work alone, in pairs, or in small groups.

2. As students work, note their solution strategies. Do they draw, count by ones, skip-count, or add to find the total?

Debrief

1. What total did you find? How did you find it?

2. Could you find the answer a different way?

3. How might making a drawing help you find the total number?

4. How might skip-counting help you solve this problem?

Differentiate ◯ ▣

Some students may find the multiplicative relationship (that there are the same number in each bag) challenging and just add the three numbers given in the problem. Making a drawing can help students see the repeated groups. Have students look at their drawings as they listen to others describe more abstract strategies for finding the total. The visual model will increase access to such thinking.

There are 3 bags of cookies.

There are 2 oatmeal and 1 peanut butter cookie in each bag.

What is the total number of cookies in these bags?

There are 4 bags of fruit.

There are 2 bananas and 2 apples in each bag.

What is the total number of pieces of fruit in these bags?

There are 3 large bags of muffins. There are 3 corn muffins, 2 blueberry muffins, and 3 bran muffins in each large bag.

There are 2 small bags of muffins. There are 2 corn muffins and 1 bran muffin in each small bag.

What is the total number of muffins in all five bags?

Salad Garden

Standard

Adds and subtracts whole numbers

Overview

Given pictures of rectangular arrangements of plants, students count equal groups to find how many plants there are.

Problem-Solving Strategies

- Count, compute, or write an equation
- Find information in a picture, list, table, graph, or diagram

Materials

- *Salad Garden* (page 53; saladgarden.pdf)
- *Student Response Form* (page 130; studentresponse.pdf) *(optional)*

Activate

1. Ask students to discuss any experiences they have had with growing or picking fruits or vegetables. Allow time for several students to respond and to build on one another's ideas.

2. Draw a picture of three rows with two circles in each row. Ask students to identify how they counted the circles. If no one suggests the idea of equal groups, ask *How could we use equal groups to count these circles?* As students suggest counting or adding the groups of one, two, or three, record the associated equations: $1 + 1 + 1 + 1 + 1 + 1 = 6$, $2 + 2 + 2 = 6$, and $3 + 3 = 6$.

Solve

1. Distribute copies of *Salad Garden* to students. Have students work in pairs or in small groups. Draw attention to the direction that indicates students are to talk with a partner about different ways to count the plants.

2. As students work, ask *How are you finding the total? Is there a different way you can find it?*

Debrief

1. How did you count the plants? What equation could you write to show this way of counting?

2. Who counted a different way? What equation could you write to show this way of counting?

3. Do you prefer to count by ones or equal groups? Why?

Differentiate ○ □ △ ☆

Some students may be familiar with multiplication. Encourage them to write multiplication equations to correspond to the pictures or show them how to do so. Collect further formative assessment data to inform instructional planning with an exit-card task such as the following: *Aisha planted four rows of pepper plants. She planted four plants in each row. How many pepper plants did Aisha plant?*

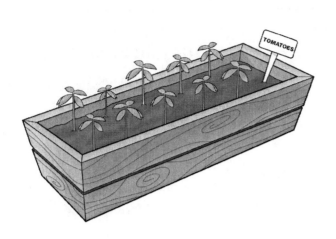

Ashish planted these tomato plants.

How many tomato plants did Ashish plant?

Talk with a partner about ways to count the plants using equal groups.

Draw a picture to show the equal groups.

Lenny planted these lettuce plants.

How many lettuce plants did Lenny plant?

Talk with a partner about ways to count the plants using equal groups. Write an equation to show one of the ways.

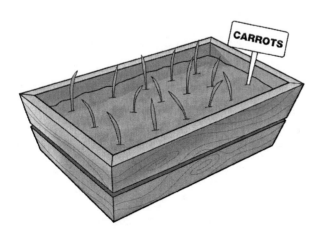

Meghan planted these carrots.

How many carrots did Meghan plant?

Write two equations to show different ways to count these carrots.

What Am I Thinking?

Standard

Adds and subtracts whole numbers

Overview

Students are given the sum and difference of two numbers and use this information to identify the numbers.

Problem-Solving Strategies

- Guess and check or make an estimate
- Organize information in a picture, list, table, graph, or diagram
- Use logical reasoning

Materials

- *What Am I Thinking?* (page 55; thinking.pdf)
- *Student Response Form* (page 130; studentresponse.pdf) *(optional)*

Activate

1. Dramatize being a mind reader. Tell students to think of two numbers less than 10. Have them record the numbers and show them to a neighbor. Call on a student and say that with only two clues, you will read his or her mind and determine the numbers. Ask the student to tell you the sum of the numbers, then ask for the difference. Ask if the student's neighbor agrees with these answers. (Give time for the neighbor to check.) Tell the numbers with dramatic flair and have the student's neighbor read aloud the numbers that were written to validate your response.

2. Repeat this activity several times and then ask, *How do you think I am doing this? What if I tell you the sum of my numbers is 10 and their difference is 6? Can you "read my mind"?*

Solve

1. Distribute copies of *What Am I Thinking?* to students. Have students work alone, in pairs, or in small groups.

2. As students work, note their strategies. If they guess, does their guess suggest good number sense? If they guess randomly, does that guess inform their next guess? Do they make a list of guesses that they make or repeat guesses? Do they make a list of addends for the sum?

Debrief

1. What strategy did you use?

2. How could making a guess help you? How might you decide on a guess to make?

3. How could making a list help?

Differentiate ◯ ◻ △ ☆

Meet with a small group of students who are unsure of how guesses can be used to solve these types of problems. Encourage them to guess two numbers with that sum and then check their difference. Show them how to keep track of their guesses and their checks by recording them in a list or table. If you wish to assign an exit card consider the following: *In all, two sisters have 14 shells. The older sister has 2 more shells than the younger sister. How many shells does each sister have?*

I am thinking of two numbers.

When I add the numbers, I get 12.

When I subtract them, I get 2.

What are my numbers?

_____ and _____

I am thinking of two numbers.

When I add the numbers, I get 20.

When I subtract them, I get 10.

What are my numbers?

_____ and _____

I am thinking of two numbers.

When I add the numbers, I get 30.

When I subtract them, I get 14.

What are my numbers?

_____ and _____

Same Sums

Standards

- Adds and subtracts whole numbers
- Understands the inverse relationship between addition and subtraction

Overview

Students must place given numbers in a graphic design so that the sum of each set of three numbers is the same.

Problem-Solving Strategies

- Count, compute, or write an equation
- Find information in a picture, list, table, graph, or diagram
- Guess and check or make an estimate
- Use logical reasoning

Materials

- *Same Sums* (page 57; samesums.pdf)
- sticky notes (*optional*)
- calculators (*optional*)
- *Student Response Form* (page 130; studentresponse.pdf) (*optional*)

Activate

1. Display the numbers 7, 12, 5, and 18 and write _____ + _____ + 10 = 22 on the board. Have students talk with a partner about which two of the numbers should be written in the blanks to make the equation true. (*7 and 5*)

2. Have students identify the numbers and discuss their strategies. If no one mentions checking their sums or thinking about subtraction, ask *How do you know you found the right numbers? How might knowing that 22 – 10 = 12 help you find the numbers?*

Solve

1. Distribute copies of *Same Sums* to students and review the directions. Have students work alone, in pairs, or in small groups.

2. As the students work, ask *Why are you trying these numbers? What did you learn from your guess that did not have the correct sum?*

Debrief

1. Where did you put the numbers? Is there someplace else they could go?

2. Which number did you place first? Why?

3. What strategies did you use to solve the problem?

Differentiate ◯

Some students may find it helpful to write the numbers on sticky notes and move them around to check the sums of different combinations of numbers. You may also wish to allow students to use calculators to find the sums, enabling them to focus more on the logical thinking involved in deciding which sums to check.

Write each number from the box in one of the squares.

Each set of three numbers in a line must have a sum of 25.

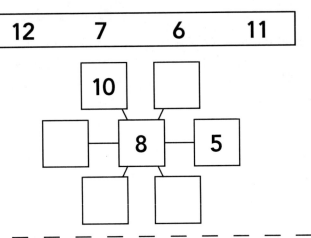

Write each number from the box in one of the squares.

Each set of three numbers in a line must have a sum of 50.

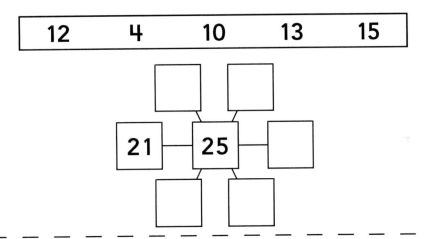

Write each number from the box in one of the squares.

Each set of three numbers in a line must have a sum of 100.

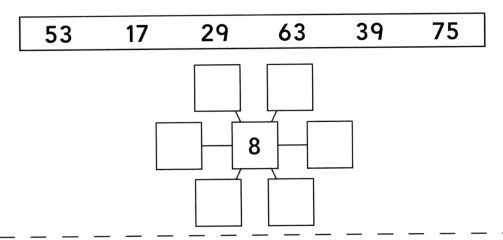

Puzzlers

Standards

- Adds and subtracts whole numbers
- Understands the inverse relationship between addition and subtraction

Overview

Students complete a sequence of computational steps and arrive back at the original number, reinforcing the inverse relationship between addition and subtraction.

Problem-Solving Strategies

- Count, compute, or write an equation
- Generalize a pattern

Materials

- *Puzzlers* (page 59; puzzlers.pdf)
- carrel or heavy book
- counters or base-ten blocks
- *Student Response Form* (page 130; studentresponse.pdf) *(optional)*

Activate

1. Ask students what they know about how addition is related to subtraction. Record student responses.

2. Call on a student volunteer. Set up a carrel or book to create a screen between you and the student. Direct the volunteer to take 1–10 counters, without telling you the number chosen, and place them behind the screen. Have the other students silently count to find the amount the student chose and to remember that number. Give the student the following directions, allowing time for implementation after each direction: *Add six more counters. Take away one counter. Take away five more counters. Now, tell me how many counters you have.* Dramatize thinking seriously until you announce that the student has the same number of counters with which he or she started (say the number).

3. You may wish to have students discuss with partners how you were able to tell the original number of counters, but do not debrief as a whole group. Many students will have more ideas after solving a similar problem.

Solve

1. Distribute copies of *Puzzlers* to students. Have students work alone, in pairs, or in small groups.

2. Note whether students automatically recognize the answer or compute to find it.

Debrief

1. Why do the numbers end up the same? Can anyone explain that a different way?

2. How do these answers relate to the list we made about addition and subtraction?

3. What other problem could you create that would be like this?

Differentiate ⬤ ◻

Some students may need to visualize the changes in value. Make counters or base-ten blocks available for students to model the computations. Supporting students' use of manipulatives, mental computation skills, or pencil and paper techniques validates a wide range of learners.

Step 1: Start with 20.

Step 2: Add 7.

Step 3: Subtract 7.

What number do you get?

Choose a different start number and follow steps 2 and 3 in the box.

What number do you get?

Why do you think this happens?

Step 1: Start with 41.

Step 2: Subtract 19.

Step 3: Add 21.

Step 4: Subtract 2.

What number do you get?

Choose a different start number and follow steps 2–4 in the box.

What number do you get?

Why do you think this happens?

Step 1: Start with 65.

Step 2: Subtract 29.

Step 3: Subtract 3.

Step 4: Add 15.

Step 5: Add 17.

What number do you get?

Choose a different start number and follow steps 2–5 in the box.

What number do you get?

Why do you think this happens?

Puzzlers

Animal Stories

Standard

Solves real-world problems involving addition and subtraction of whole numbers

Overview

In this problem set, students complete story problems by writing missing numbers. The numbers the students choose must make mathematical sense.

Problem-Solving Strategies

- Act it out or use manipulatives
- Use logical reasoning

Materials

- *Animal Stories* (page 61; animal.pdf)
- *Student Response Form* (page 130; studentresponse.pdf) *(optional)*

Activate

1. Ask students where they see animals and what kinds of animals they see there. Allow several students to respond.

2. Display the following problem for students:

   Camille saw grasshoppers, crickets,

   and butterflies in the garden. She saw

   _____ grasshoppers, _____
   $\quad$ A $\qquad\qquad\qquad\qquad$ B

   crickets, and _____ *butterflies. Camille*
   $\qquad\qquad\qquad$ C

   saw _____ *insects in all.*
   $\qquad$ D

   Have students talk with a neighbor about what numbers to put on the lines so that the story makes sense.

3. Have a few students share their solutions. Help students note the similarities and differences among their answers by asking questions such as *Can A be greater than B? Can A be greater than D? What must be true about D?*

Solve

1. Distribute copies of *Animal Stories* to students. Have students work alone or in pairs.

2. As students work, ask *What can you do to make sure these numbers make sense? Do you think you found the only numbers that will work?*

Debrief

1. How did you decide what numbers to write? Did someone use a different strategy?

2. Are there different numbers that could be used?

3. What is the same about these different numbers?

Differentiate ☐ △

The numbers students choose may indicate their confidence levels, especially if their chosen numbers are particularly small or large. In the on-level and above-level problems, students may be distracted by the number that states a comparison and include it in their sums. Ask these students *How can we keep track of the numbers that tell how many animals are in each group?*

Write numbers on the lines to create a story that makes sense.

Manny saw _____ animals at a small farm.   A = _____
A

The animals were all goats, cows, or sheep.   B = _____

He saw _____ goats, _____ sheep, and   C = _____
B   C

_____ cows.   D = _____
D

Write numbers on the lines to create a story that makes sense.

Jamie held _____ animals at the pet store.   A = _____
A

She held mice, hamsters, and guinea pigs at   B = _____

the pet store. She held _____ more guinea   C = _____
B

pigs than mice. Jamie held _____ guinea   D = _____
C

pigs and _____ mice. Jamie also held   E = _____
D

_____ hamsters.
E

Write numbers on the lines to create a story that makes sense.

Benito saw _____ dogs at the dog park.   A = _____
A

He saw _____ poodles. He saw _____   B = _____
B   C

fewer poodles than beagles. He saw _____   C = _____
D

beagles. He saw _____ bull dogs. The   D = _____
E

rest of the dogs were collies. Benito saw   E = _____

_____ collies.   F = _____
F

Number Blocks

Standards

- Understands symbolic, concrete, and pictorial representations of numbers
- Solves real-world problems involving addition and subtraction of whole numbers

Overview

Students are shown a number represented with base-ten blocks. New blocks are added to the set and students write the numeral for the new number that is represented.

Problem-Solving Strategies

- Act it out or use manipulatives
- Count, compute, or write an equation
- Find information in a picture, list, table, graph, or diagram

Materials

- *Number Blocks* (page 63; blocks.pdf)
- base-ten blocks
- *Student Response Form* (page 130; studentresponse.pdf) *(optional)*

Activate

1. Distribute base-ten blocks to students and have them represent the number 124. Ask students how many tens they used to make this number, and how many ones. Tell students to add one more ten. Ask *What number do the blocks show now? How do you know?* Encourage a number of different responses, such as *I counted the one hundred, three tens, and four ones; I counted ten, twenty, thirty; I added ten to 124; or I just made the tens one more.*

2. Follow the same procedure outlined in step 1, but this time begin with the number 257 and encourage students to predict the outcome before adding another hundred block to the group.

3. Instruct students to use the blocks to show the number 352. Ask students what they would need to add to show the number 372. (Write 372 for students to see.) Ask students to explain their thinking.

Solve

1. Distribute copies of *Number Blocks* to students. Have students work alone, in pairs, or in small groups.

2. Make sure base-ten blocks are available so students can model the situations.

Debrief

1. How did you find what number the blocks show? What equation could you write to represent this situation?

2. How did you decide which blocks were needed? What equation could you write to represent this situation?

3. How does acting out a problem situation help you find the answer?

Differentiate △

For a greater challenge, encourage students to be ready to solve the problems with mental images or computations rather than by using manipulatives.

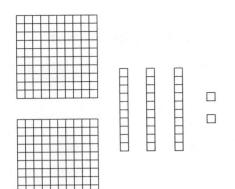

Tatiana has these hundreds, tens, and ones. She gets 2 more tens. What number does Tatiana's blocks show now?

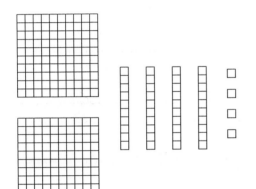

Lou has these hundreds, tens, and ones. He gets 2 more tens and 3 more ones. What number does Lou's blocks show now?

Next, Lou wants to show the number 479. What other blocks does Lou need?

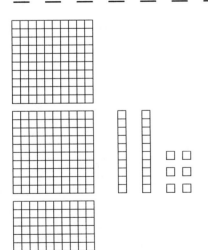

Misha has these hundreds, tens, and ones.

Beth has 6 tens and 3 ones.

Beth gives her blocks to Misha.

Misha wants to show the number 689. What other blocks does Misha need?

Figure It

Standards

- Adds and subtracts whole numbers
- Understands the inverse relationship between addition and subtraction
- Recognizes regularities in a variety of contexts

Overview

This problem set represents equations with shapes as place holders for numbers. Students identify numbers that make the equations true.

Problem-Solving Strategies

- Count, compute, or write an equation
- Guess and check or make an estimate
- Use logical reasoning

Materials

- *Figure It* (page 65; figureit.pdf)
- *Student Response Form* (page 130; studentresponse.pdf) *(optional)*

Activate

1. Display the equation $\square + \square = 16$ for students and tell them that each square stands for the same number. Ask students how they could figure out the value of the square. Several students may recognize that $8 + 8 = 16$ and say they just know the answer. Probe deeper by asking, *What could you suggest to a friend who did not recognize this fact?*

2. Display $\square + \bigcirc = 34$. Ask *Since we know the square is equal to eight, what is the value of the circle?* (26) Have students talk with partners and then share answers as a group.

Solve

1. Distribute copies of *Figure It* to students and explain that their job is to find the value of each shape. Remind them that the same shape stands for the same number.

2. Have students work in pairs or in small groups so that they can talk about their thinking. As they work, pay particular attention to how students communicate about the relationship between addition and subtraction.

Debrief

1. Who can show us how they found their answer?

2. Could there be another number that would work?

3. How can making a guess help us to make a better guess next time?

Differentiate ⬤ ⬛

Some students make random guesses. Ask questions to help them note what they can learn from their guesses that are incorrect. For example, say *I see you guessed five. Did you get a sum that was too small or too large with that guess? Will your next guess be less than five or greater than five?* Other students may be reluctant to guess and thus do not get the opportunity to learn from their guesses. Encourage such students by saying *Let's just pick a number and try it. Maybe we can learn something from our guess.*

Find the value of each shape. The same shape has the same value.

$$\bigotimes + \bigotimes = 12 \qquad \bigotimes + \triangle = 37$$

$$\bigotimes = \underline{\qquad} \qquad \triangle = \underline{\qquad}$$

Find the value of each shape. The same shape has the same value.

$$\bigcirc + \bigcirc + \bigcirc = 6 \qquad \bigcirc + \star = 131$$

$$\bigcirc = \underline{\qquad} \qquad \star = \underline{\qquad}$$

Find the value of each shape. The same shape has the same value.

$$\bowtie + \smile = 100 \qquad \smile + 16 = \bowtie$$

$$\bowtie = \underline{\qquad} \qquad \smile = \underline{\qquad}$$

Predict the Number

Standards

- Recognizes regularities in a variety of contexts
- Extends simple patterns

Overview

Students are shown the top rows of a hundred chart or a thousand chart and asked to predict a number on the chart in a position that is not shown. Then, they are asked to create and answer their own questions about the charts.

Problem-Solving Strategies

- Count, compute, or write an equation
- Find information in a picture, list, table, graph, or diagram
- Generalize a pattern

Materials

- *Predict the Number* (page 67; predict.pdf)
- hundred chart
- *Student Response Form* (page 130; studentresponse.pdf) *(optional)*

Activate

1. Display a hundred chart for students. Ask them what patterns they see. Encourage several students to share patterns they find.

2. Identify a number such as 13 and ask what is ten more than this number. *(23)*

3. Chose a new number and repeat step 2.

4. Point to a column and have students read aloud the numbers in that column. Ask students what they notice about the numbers they read. *(They increase by 10.)* Repeat with another column.

5. Review with students what it means to predict. Then, have students close their eyes. Tell them to think about where 15 is on the chart, then go down one row. Ask if they can predict what number they will see there when they open their eyes.

Solve

1. Distribute copies of *Predict the Number* to students and tell them they are going to make more predictions. Have students work in pairs or in small groups.

2. Listen for accountable talk. How do students explain their thinking to one another? Do they think in terms of tens and ones or just ones?

Debrief

1. How did you find the answer?

2. Did anyone find the answer a different way?

3. How did you keep track of your moves around the chart?

Differentiate ◯

Some students may need a copy of a hundred chart to answer the questions. Provide them with the chart, but encourage them to predict the number first and then check the chart.

1	2	3	4	5	6	7	8	9	10
11	12	13	14	15	16	17	18	19	20

Start at 17.

Go three rows down.

The number is _____.

Write your own prediction question about this chart and answer it.

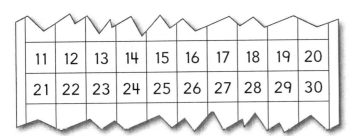

11	12	13	14	15	16	17	18	19	20
21	22	23	24	25	26	27	28	29	30

Start at 23.

Go four rows down.

Then, go six spaces to the right.

The number is_____.

Write your own prediction question about this chart and answer it.

10	20	30	40	50	60	70	80	90	100
110	120	130	140	150	160	170	180	190	200

Start at 180.

Go five rows down.

Then, go four spaces to the left.

The number is _____.

Write your own prediction question about this chart and answer it.

Living on Main Street

Standards

- Understands symbolic, concrete, and pictorial representations of numbers
- Uses base-ten concepts to compare and represent whole numbers in flexible ways

Overview

In this problem set students write missing numbers so that stories make sense.

Problem-Solving Strategies

- Find information in a picture, list, table, graph, or diagram
- Use logical reasoning

Materials

- *Living on Main Street* (page 69; mainstreet.pdf)
- *Student Response Form* (page 130; studentresponse.pdf) (*optional*)

Activate

1. Display the numbers 231, 239, and 235 for students. Ask them how these numbers are the same. Encourage students to offer several ideas. For example, if one student notes that the numbers are all in the two hundreds, ask what else can be said about the size of the numbers. Ask what they can say about all of the numbers using the terms *greater than*, *less than*, and *between*. Ask questions to solicit ideas that have not been mentioned and to review academic vocabulary. For example, you might ask *What do you notice about the tens place? How many digits do these numbers have?*

2. Direct students to choose one of the numbers. Ask *Without naming the number, what can you tell us about it so we will know which number you chose?*

3. Remind students that we see numbers every day on houses, apartments, and businesses. Ask them why these buildings have numbers.

Solve

1. Distribute copies of *Living on Main Street* to students. Direct students to the numbers in the boxes that represent house numbers. Tell students that their task is to use the clues to find each person's house number on Main Street. Have students work alone, in pairs, or in small groups.

2. As students work, ask clarifying questions, such as *Why did you choose this number? What size number do you think goes best here?*

Debrief

1. What house number did you find? How did you decide it was the number?

2. Is there a different solution path?

3. How can crossing off numbers be helpful?

Differentiate ○ □ △ ☆

Students with a particular interest in these types of problems may wish to create similar problems using their own house numbers. Have pairs of students write problems together, exchange them with another pair, and solve the new problems.

| 135 | 536 | 152 | 125 |

What is Delilah's house number?

The number is greater than 130.

It is less than 158.

There is a 5 in the ones place.

Delilah lives at _____ Main Street.

| 257 | 245 | 262 | 258 |

What is Hector's house number?

The number is less than 260.

The number has a 5 in the tens place.

It is not equal to 250 + 8.

Hector lives at _____ Main Street.

| 529 | 584 | 592 | 565 | 538 |

What is Ava's house number?

The number is between 530 and 590.

The three digits have a sum of 16.

The number is not equal to 500 + 60 + 5.

Ava lives at _____ Main Street.

Machine Math

Standards
- Adds and subtracts whole numbers
- Understands the inverse relationship between addition and subtraction

Overview
Students are shown input and output values. They find the relationship between these values and use that pattern to find missing values.

Problem-Solving Strategies
- Count, compute, or write an equation
- Find information in a picture, list, table, graph, or diagram
- Generalize a pattern

Materials
- *Machine Math* (page 71; machine.pdf)
- chart paper
- calculators *(optional)*
- *Student Response Form* (page 130; studentresponse.pdf) *(optional)*

Activate
1. Put students in groups of four to five for a round-robin activity. Set up T-charts labeled *In* and *Out* around the room. Have students in each group count off to determine the order in which they will participate. Tell students that their task is to add five to each number you say. For example, call the first students to go to their group's chart and write 52 in the *In* column. Then, those students add five to this number and write 57 in the *Out* column. These students return to their groups, the second students go to the chart. Again, say a number for them to write in the *In* column and have them write the number that is five more in the *Out* column. Repeat until each student has gone to the chart twice.

2. Ask *What is the difference between each number pair in the two columns? If the number 150 were written in the* Out *column, what number would be in the* In *column?*

Solve
1. Distribute copies of *Machine Math* to students. Have students work alone or in pairs.

2. Remind students that each machine does the same operation to each number, so they should check their computation if they are finding differences that are not the same.

Debrief
1. How did you find the missing numbers?

2. What is this machine doing to all of the numbers? How can you explain what is happening in words? How can you show it using symbols?

Differentiate
If students are not able to compute accurately, they will not be able to find the pattern between the *In* and *Out* numbers. You may want to allow students to check their computations with calculators if they are not finding a consistent difference between the columns.

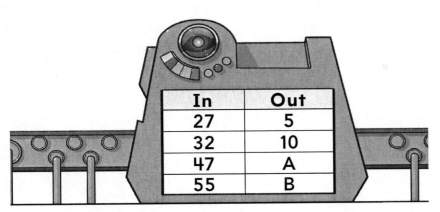

In	Out
27	5
32	10
47	A
55	B

A = _____
B = _____

Write a sentence to describe what this machine does.

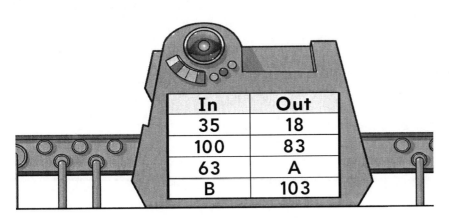

In	Out
35	18
100	83
63	A
B	103

A = _____
B = _____

Write a sentence to describe what this machine does.

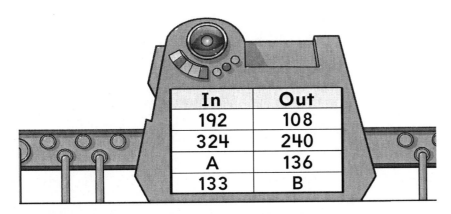

In	Out
192	108
324	240
A	136
133	B

A = _____
B = _____

Write a sentence to describe what this machine does.

Show It

Standards

- Understands symbolic, concrete, and pictorial representations of numbers
- Uses base-ten concepts to compare and represent whole numbers in flexible ways

Overview

Students are shown a collection of base-ten blocks and asked what numbers they could show using some or all of the blocks. Students record the standard numerals for each number they can create.

Problem-Solving Strategies

- Find information in a picture, list, table, graph, or diagram
- Organize information in a picture, list, table, graph, or diagram

Materials

- *Show It* (page 73; showit.pdf)
- base-ten blocks
- *Student Response Form* (page 130; studentresponse.pdf) *(optional)*

Activate

1. Display two hundreds, two tens, and three ones base-ten blocks, each in a separate group. Ask a volunteer to take at least one block from each group. Have the student show the other students these blocks and write the number represented. For example, if the student took one hundred, one ten, and two ones, he or she would write 112.

2. Repeat step 1 with other volunteers, asking them to take a different set of blocks each time.

Solve

1. Distribute copies of *Show It* to students. Have base-ten blocks available for students to use. Have students work alone, in pairs, or in small groups.

2. As students work, you may want to ask clarifying and refocusing questions, such as *What number are you showing now? What will you try next? Why?*

Debrief

1. How did you find your answers?

2. Do you think you found all the numbers? Why or why not?

3. Is there another way to organize the numbers you found?

4. What numbers could you show if you could use all of the blocks?

Differentiate ⬤

Allowing students to find their own ways to organize data helps them to become more independent problem solvers. At this level, it is all right if they do not identify all the possibilities. If some students require more structure for success, you might start a table for them (with headings of *Hundreds*, *Tens*, and *Ones*), which they can complete.

You have:

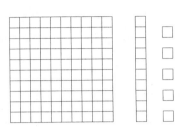

Use hundreds, tens, and ones blocks. Use at least one of each kind of block.

What numbers can you show?

You have:

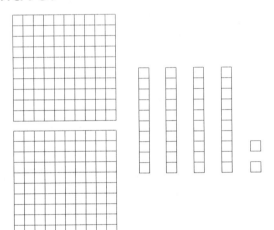

Use hundreds, tens, and ones blocks. Use at least one of each kind of block.

Use more tens than hundreds.

What numbers can you show?

You have:

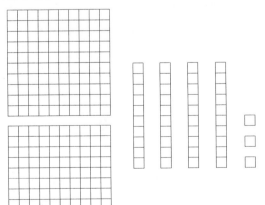

Use hundreds, tens, and ones blocks. Use at least one of each kind of block.

Use fewer ones than tens.

What numbers can you show?

Where Is It?

Standards

- Counts whole numbers
- Understands symbolic, concrete, and pictorial representations of numbers
- Adds and subtracts whole numbers

Overview

Students are given number lines with a specific number on the line identified. Students use this information to identify another given location on the line. Then, they find a number 10, 100, or 110 more than the number they identified.

Problem-Solving Strategies

- Count, compute, or write an equation
- Find information in a picture, list, table, graph, or diagram

Materials

- *Where Is It?* (page 75; whereisit.pdf)
- *Number Line 0–30* (numberline30.pdf)
- *Number Line 0–300* (numberline300.pdf)
- *Student Response Form* (page 130; studentresponse.pdf) *(optional)*

Activate

1. Have students count, in chorus, to 30 by ones. Then, have them count from 10 to 200 by tens.

2. Display *Number Line 0–30* for students. Ask them what they notice about the hash marks where the tens are. Point to a few positions on the number line adjacent to a tens mark and have students identify the corresponding numbers.

3. Display *Number Line 0–300* for students. Ask them what the hash marks between the hundreds show. Point to a few positions adjacent to the hundreds on the number line and have students identify the numbers indicated.

Solve

1. Distribute copies of *Where Is It?* to students. Have students work alone, in pairs, or in small groups.

2. Observe students as they work. Do they count each line or recognize the importance of the longer hash marks?

Debrief

1. How did you identify the number indicated by the question mark?

2. Did anyone use a different strategy?

3. How did you identify the value of the number that is 10 (or 100 or 110) more than that number?

Differentiate ◯

Make copies of the number lines for students to refer to throughout this activity. Being able to move their fingers along the line can be helpful to many students.

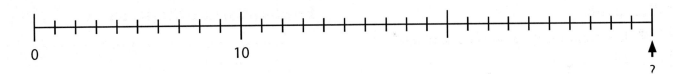

? = _____

What is 10 more than this number?

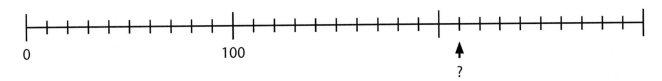

? = _____

What is 100 more than this number?

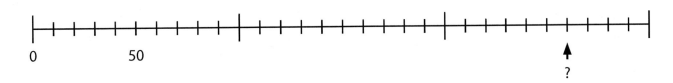

? = _____

What is 110 more than this number?

Finish the Equations

Standards

- Adds and subtracts whole numbers
- Understands basic estimation strategies

Overview

Students are provided with a set of numbers they must arrange to complete equations. Students might estimate as well as focus on the tens or ones digits to limit the amount of trial and error.

Problem-Solving Strategies

- Count, compute, or write an equation
- Guess and check or make an estimate
- Simplify the problem

Materials

- *Finish the Equations* (page 77; finishequations.pdf)
- *Student Response Form* (page 130; studentresponse.pdf) *(optional)*

Activate

1. Review the terms *sum* and *difference* with students. These words can be confused with *some* and *different*. Write the terms on the board and have students provide informal definitions.

2. Display the following numbers for students: 23, 7, 10, and 53. Have students record the numbers as well. Direct the students to look for two numbers whose sum is 33. *(23 and 10)* Ask students how they found the numbers. Have several students respond so that a variety of approaches are identified. Though many students may report that they guessed and checked or "just knew them," probe deeper by asking *Did you include 53 in one of your guesses? Why or why not? How might looking at the tens digits help you find the numbers?*

3. Repeat the process in step 2, asking students to find two numbers that have a difference of 30. *(53 and 23)*

Solve

1. Distribute copies of *Finish the Equations* to students. Have students work alone or in pairs.

2. As students work, note the guesses they make. Do they suggest good number sense?

Debrief

1. If a number can only be used once, how can this rule help you find the answers?

2. What equations did you find easiest to complete? Why were they easier?

3. What ideas might we put on a list of ways to help us find these sums and differences?

Differentiate ● ■

Some students may be overwhelmed by all of the possible combinations. In problems where each number can be used only once, encourage students to cross off numbers when they are used. This process will simplify the problem by helping students focus on the more limited choices for the following equation.

Use each number from the box once to write true equations.

7	15	30	2

$37 = \underline{\hspace{1cm}} + \underline{\hspace{1cm}}$

$\underline{\hspace{1cm}} - \underline{\hspace{1cm}} = 13$

Use each number from the box once to write true equations.

4	34	125	10	6	48

$82 = \underline{\hspace{1cm}} + \underline{\hspace{1cm}}$

$\underline{\hspace{1cm}} - 119 = \underline{\hspace{1cm}}$

$\underline{\hspace{1cm}} + \underline{\hspace{1cm}} = 14$

Use each number from the box at least once to write true equations.

147	121	136	116

$283 = \underline{\hspace{1cm}} + \underline{\hspace{1cm}}$

$\underline{\hspace{1cm}} - 31 = \underline{\hspace{1cm}}$

$257 - \underline{\hspace{1cm}} = \underline{\hspace{1cm}}$

Ring Toss

Standards

- Understands symbolic, concrete, and pictorial representations of numbers
- Uses base-ten concepts to compare and represent whole numbers in flexible ways
- Adds and subtracts whole numbers

Overview

A ring toss board is pictured in which tosses can score 1, 10, or 100 point(s). Rings have landed on the board and students must determine the total value of the tosses. They also determine the total score after additional points are scored.

Problem-Solving Strategies

- Find information in a picture, list, table, graph, or diagram
- Organize information in a picture, list, table, graph, model or diagram

Materials

- *Ring Toss* (page 79; ringtoss.pdf)
- *Ring Toss Template* (ringtosstemplate.pdf)
- *Student Response Form* (page 130; studentresponse.pdf) *(optional)*

Activate

1. Ask students if they have ever played a ring toss game. Provide time for a few students who have done so to describe the game and tell where they played it. Alternatively, you could have a student dramatize playing the game and have the students guess the game the student was demonstrating.

2. Display or distribute copies of *Ring Toss Template*. Ask *If I tossed three rings and got three points, where did the rings land? What if I got 21 points? What if I got 120 points?*

Solve

1. Distribute copies of *Ring Toss* to students. Have students look at the boards and note that tosses have already been made. Have students work alone or in pairs.

2. As the students work, observe how they find the total number of points. What evidence do you see of their understanding of place value?

Debrief

1. How did you find the total points for the rings shown? Did anyone find the total a different way?

2. How did you find the total after the player got more points? Did anyone find the total a different way?

3. How might someone use a drawing to find the total?

Differentiate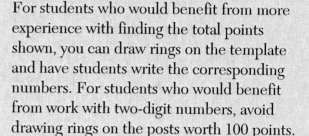

For students who would benefit from more experience with finding the total points shown, you can draw rings on the template and have students write the corresponding numbers. For students who would benefit from work with two-digit numbers, avoid drawing rings on the posts worth 100 points.

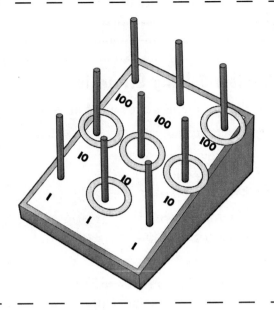

Chris tossed these rings. How many points does Chris have?

He gets another 10 points. How many points does Chris have now?

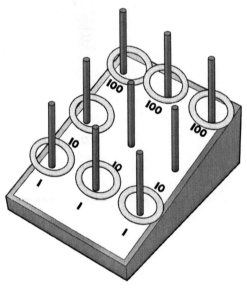

Angelo tossed these rings. Then, he gets 14 more points. How many points does Angelo have now?

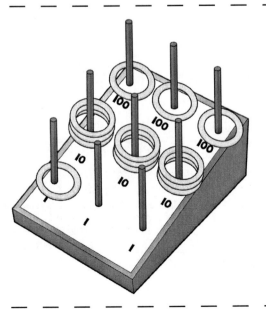

Jamila tossed these rings. Then, she tossed one more ring and it landed on a peg. How many total points could Jamila have now? Find all the possible totals.

Counting Along

Standards

- Recognizes regularities in a variety of contexts
- Extends simple patterns

Overview

This problem set focuses on skip-counting by 2, 5, or 10 and on forming generalizations.

Problem-Solving Strategies

- Count, compute, or write an equation
- Generalize a pattern
- Use logical reasoning

Materials

- *Counting Along* (page 81; countingalong.pdf)
- counters
- *Student Response Form* (page 130; studentresponse.pdf) *(optional)*

Activate

1. Organize a round-robin with students in groups of four or five. Distribute counters and one sheet of paper to each group. Have students count off in their small groups (1–4 or 1–5). In this order, they take turns going to the board to write the next number they would say when counting by two. At the same time, the other students place a set of two counters on the piece of paper. So, first all of the number 1 students go to the board and write 2 as the remaining students place two counters on the paper. Next, the number 2 students write the next number they would say when they count by two (4) as another set of two counters is added to the paper. Have students continue until they reach 16. As students rotate, note who can write the next number readily, who counts up to write the number, and who relies on a friend for help.

2. Ask *How many numbers did we write when we counted by twos to 16?* Then, have the students count the groups of twos as they confirm that there are 16 counters on their papers.

Solve

1. Distribute copies of *Counting Along* to students. Have students work alone, in pairs, or in small groups.

2. If necessary, ask *How can you use your first count to help you make a prediction?*

Debrief

1. What did you think about to help you make a prediction?

2. What patterns did you find?

Differentiate ⬤

Make counters available for those students who wish to use them to identify the next number they say when skip-counting. You may want to have some students work with partners where one student says the numbers and the other student makes a tally mark for each number said.

Count by two to 10. Write the numbers you say.

Predict how many numbers you will say if you start over and count by two to 20. Explain your answer.

Say and count the numbers to check. How many did you get?

Count by ten to 100. Write the numbers you say.

Predict how many numbers will you say if you start over and count by ten to 300. Explain your answer.

Say and count the numbers to check. How many did you get?

Count by five to 50. Write the numbers you say.

Predict how many numbers you will say if you start over and count by five to 400. Explain your answer.

Say and count the numbers to check. How many did you get?

The Lee Family

Standard

Understands that numerals are symbols used to represent quantities or attributes of real-world objects

Overview

Students are given stories with missing numerical information along with the missing numbers. Students must decide where to write the numbers so that the story makes sense.

Problem-Solving Strategies

- Guess and check or make an estimate
- Use logical reasoning

Materials

- *The Lee Family* (page 83; leefamily.pdf)
- *Student Response Form* (page 130; studentresponse.pdf) *(optional)*

Activate

1. Display the problem below for students. Read the story aloud once (saying *blank* for the places where the missing numbers go) and then have students read it aloud with you.

3	576	10	9

   Jenny is ____ years old and looking forward to her ____th birthday next month. She lives at ____ Elm Street and has ____ sisters.

2. Have students talk in pairs or small groups about where the numbers should go so that the story makes sense. (9; 10; 576; 3)

3. Have the pairs or groups report to the class about where they think the numbers should be placed and why they think so. Ask questions to clarify their thinking, such as *Is there any other place where 576 would make sense? How did you find out how old Jenny is now?*

Solve

1. Distribute copies of *The Lee Family* to students. Have students work in pairs or in small groups.

2. Listen to the conversations among students. What reasons do they give for their choices? To refocus students, you might ask *Which number is greatest? Where might such a large number be placed?*

Debrief

1. Which number was the easiest to place? Why did you think so?

2. Do you have to arrange the numbers in order? Why might you *not* want to do this?

3. Which blanks were hardest to fill? Why?

Differentiate ○ □ △ ☆

Some students may need to establish their own ideas before talking with others. Provide a place for such students to work quietly. Invite them to join a pair or group once they are ready to share.

Use each number from the box once to create a story that makes sense.

16	11	132	14

The Lee family lives at _____ Spring Trail. Bolin is the oldest boy in his family. He is _____ years old. His brother, Jin, is ____ years old. Bolin's older sister, Ming, is _____ years old.

Use each number from the box once to create a story that makes sense.

142	5	8	99	100

Ming is one of the stars of the girls' basketball team at her school. There have been ____ games so far this year. Ming has scored a total of ____ points. Ming helps take care of her great-grandmother who is ____ years old and looking forward to her ____th birthday. Ming also babysits for Sara, who lives next door. Sara is in kindergarten and is ____ years old.

Use each number from the box once to create a story that makes sense.

950	100	50	5	850	54

Mr. Lee travels a lot for work. This week he has flown ____ miles. Mrs. Lee has flown ____ more miles than Mr. Lee this week, or ____ total miles. In the last ____ years, Mr. and Mrs. Lee have been to all of the ____ states in the United States. Mr. Lee's birthday is next week. He will be ____ years old.

From the Beginning

Standards

- Adds and subtracts whole numbers
- Understands the inverse relationship between addition and subtraction

Overview

Students are given the answer that results from two computations and must identify the beginning number.

Problem-Solving Strategies

- Count, compute, or write an equation
- Guess and check or make an estimate
- Simplify the problem
- Work backward

Materials

- *From the Beginning* (page 85; fromthebeginning.pdf)
- *Student Response Form* (page 130; studentresponse.pdf) *(optional)*

Activate

1. Show students the equation $\square + 6 = 18$ and have them determine the missing number. *(12)* Encourage them to explain their strategies.

2. Repeat the activity with the equation $\square - 7 = 29$. *(36)*

3. Repeat the activity with a more complex equation such as $\square + 6 - 4 = 23$. *(21)*

Solve

1. Distribute copies of *From the Beginning* to students. Have students work alone, in pairs, or in small groups.

2. Refocus students as necessary by asking them to show you how they got from one step to another step.

Debrief

1. What did you find for the starting number? How did you find it?

2. Did anyone use a different strategy?

3. How might we combine the middle steps? How would this be helpful?

4. How can we check our answers?

5. Why do you think some people call these *working backward* problems?

Differentiate ⬤ ▢ △ ☆

Though guessing and checking is not as efficient as working backward, it does help students to better understand the relationships among the numbers. You may want to suggest that some students simplify the problem by using smaller numbers. Once they recognize the relationships among those numbers, students can apply the ideas to the greater numbers. If you wish to assign an exit-card task, consider the following: *Aiden is thinking of a number. When he subtracts 43 from the number he gets 68. What number is Aiden thinking about?*

Determine the starting number.

| ? | − | 100 | − | 1 | = | 24 |

? = _____

Determine the starting number.

| ? | − | 50 | + | 25 | = | 150 |

? = _____

Determine the starting number.

| ? | + | 220 | − | 175 | = | 325 |

? = _____

#50774—50 Leveled Math Problems, Level 2   **85**

All About Us

Standards

- Counts whole numbers
- Collects and represents information about objects or events in simple graphs

Overview

Students respond to questions by finding the appropriate information in picture graphs. Interpretation of the questions and counting the graphic symbols are emphasized.

Problem-Solving Strategies

- Count, compute, or write an equation
- Find information in a picture, list, table, graph, or diagram

Materials

- *All About Us* (page 87; allaboutus.pdf)
- sticky dots
- chart paper
- *Student Response Form* (page 130; studentresponse.pdf) *(optional)*

Activate

1. Survey students on a topic of particular interest to them. For example, you might identify types of games, titles of books, or sports. On chart paper, write the question *Which Do You Like Best?* as the title for a picture graph and list four choices.

2. Distribute one sticky dot to each student. Have students place their sticky dots on the picture graph to indicate their choice.

3. Ask questions about the graph that require students to identify the number of students who chose each category. Then, ask students to make comparisons among the choices. For example, ask which category was chosen the most.

4. Ask students how graphs help us to find the answer that was chosen least.

Solve

1. Distribute copies of *All About Us* to students and tell them that these graphs show information about other children. Have students work alone, in pairs, or in small groups. When working together, each student should count the smiley faces to ensure accuracy.

2. As you observe students at work, note those who count to find the total or difference and those who use addition and subtraction.

Debrief

1. How does the word *not* tell you what to count?

2. What did you do to help you keep track of the smiley faces when you counted them?

3. What else could you do to help you keep track?

Differentiate ⬤

As they count, some students may find it helpful to write the numbers 1, 2, 3, 4, etc., directly on the smiley faces. Students could also choose to write the totals for each row at the end of that row and then add or subtract the numbers to answer the questions.

Pets We Have   ☺ = 1 child

bird	☺☺☺☺☺☺☺
cat	☺☺☺☺☺☺☺☺☺☺☺
dog	☺☺☺☺☺☺☺☺☺☺☺☺☺☺
hamster	☺☺

How many more children have a dog than a bird for a pet?

How We Get to School   ☺ = 1 child

bike	☺☺☺☺
bus	☺☺☺☺☺☺☺
car	☺☺☺☺☺
feet	☺☺☺☺☺☺

How many children did not take the bus to school?

What Time Do You Go To Bed?   ☺ = 1 child

7:30 P.M.	☺☺☺☺☺☺☺☺☺
8:00 P.M.	☺☺☺☺☺
8:30 P.M.	☺☺☺☺☺☺☺☺☺☺☺
9:00 P.M.	☺☺☺☺☺

How many children went to bed after 7:45?

Last Names

Standards

- Makes organized lists of information necessary for solving a problem
- Understands that some events are more likely to happen than others

Overview

Given a list, students examine characteristics of their classmates' last names. They count according to the given criteria and make tally marks in a chart to summarize the information.

Problem-Solving Strategies

- Count, compute, or write an equation
- Organize information in a picture, list, table, graph, or diagram

Materials

- *Last Names* (page 89; lastnames.pdf)
- class list of students' names
- *Student Response Form* (page 130; studentresponse.pdf) *(optional)*

Activate

1. Distribute a list of students' names to students. Have students read the last names together. Ask questions such as *Whose last names begin with the letter s?* Model making a tally mark for each name that is listed. Ask *How many names are there that begin with the letter s?* If you wish, model the convention of making tallies in groups of five.

2. Have students identify the first six names on the list. Then, ask which of these names have the letter *o* in them. Again, model making tally marks for each name that has an *o* in it. Ask how many of these names have the letter *o* in them.

Solve

1. Distribute copies of *Last Names* to students. Have students work in pairs. Have one student identify the names as the other makes tally marks. Encourage students to exchange roles and repeat the task to check for accuracy.

2. Provide descriptive feedback as students work. For example, *I see you are making sure you check each name carefully.* Refocus students by asking *How could you keep track of the names you have already considered? Does it say the two letters have to be together?*

Debrief

1. What did you find out about the last names in our class?

2. Do you think most of the last names in the class next door end in *n*? Why or why not?

3. Do you think there are fewer than five last names in the class next door with the letter *a*? Why or why not?

Differentiate ⬤

You may want to provide some students with a partial list of names so that there are fewer names to consider.

Last Name Ends in N

Last Name Ends in *n*	
Last Name Does Not End in *n*	

Look at the last name of each student on the list.

Record a tally mark for each name.

How many names do not end in *n*?

Last Name Has Two of the Same Letters

No Letters the Same	
Exactly Two Letters the Same	
More Than Two Letters the Same	

Look at the last name of each student on the list.

Record a tally mark for each name.

How many names have exactly two letters the same?

Number of Letters in Last Name

Less than 5	
Between 5 and 10	
Exactly 10	
More than 10	

Look at the last name of each student on the list.

Record a tally mark in the chart for each name.

Do most of the names have 10 or more letters? Explain.

Measure It

Standards

- Knows processes for measuring length using basic standard units
- Collects and represents information about objects or events in simple graphs

Overview

Students take measurements to the nearest inch and record the measures in a line plot. Then, they answer questions about their data.

Problem-Solving Strategies

- Count, compute, or write an equation
- Organize information in a picture, list, table, graph, or diagram

Materials

- *Measure It* (page 91; measureit.pdf)
- crayons
- rulers
- *Student Response Form* (page 130; studentresponse.pdf) *(optional)*

Activate

1. Ask students what they know about how to measure something to the nearest inch. Make a list of students' ideas.

2. Display a crayon for students and explain that you are going to make a mistake in measuring it. Demonstrate various errors such as not aligning the edge of the crayon to the zero on the ruler and incorrectly rounding to the nearest inch. Then, model the correct way to measure the crayon and record its length.

3. Invite volunteers to measure several other crayons of varying lengths, and record their measurements.

4. Demonstrate creating a line plot to display the data collected about crayon lengths. Model marking an X to represent each measurement on the line plot. For example:

```
                        x
             x    x    x    x
   _____
    0    1    2    3    4    5    6
```

Solve

1. Distribute copies of *Measure It* to students. Have students work in pairs so that one student can measure while the other checks the accuracy of the process. Have students reverse roles for the next measurement they make.

2. As the students work, ask questions such as *How do you decide which is the closest inch?*

Debrief

1. How did making a line plot help you answer the questions?

2. What answer did you find? Can other answers be correct?

Differentiate △

Encourage students to find other objects to measure and collect data about. Have them create a line plot of their data and pose questions about their data.

Find 6 pencils. Measure the length of each pencil to the nearest inch. Make a line plot of your data. How many pencils were shorter than 7 inches?

```
_____
0    1    2    3    4    5    6    7    8    9    10   11
                    Number of Inches
```

Find 8 books. Measure the height of each book to the nearest inch. Make a line plot of your data. How many books are equal to or longer than 5 inches?

```
_____
0    1    2    3    4    5    6    7    8    9    10   11
                    Number of Inches
```

Measure the arm length of 10 children to the nearest inch. Make a line plot of your data. How many people have an arm length less than or equal to 15 inches?

```
_____
10   11   12   13   14   15   16   17   18   19   20   21
                    Number of Inches
```

Find the Lengths

Standard

Knows processes for measuring length using basic standard units

Overview

Students represent measurements on centimeter rulers. They use statements with the comparative terms of *shorter, longer, shortest,* and *longest* to identify which object belongs to which person and the lengths of those objects.

Problem-Solving Strategy

Find information in a picture, list, table, graph, or diagram

Materials

- *Find the Lengths* (page 93; findlengths.pdf)
- centimeter rulers
- one crayon
- *Student Response Form* (page 130; studentresponse.pdf) *(optional)*

Activate

1. Draw two lines of different lengths (each less than 12 inches) and post them on opposite sides of the room. Ask students how they could determine the longer line. After students provide a few suggestions, ask them which ways will allow them to do this without moving the lines. Have students demonstrate their techniques, which might include comparing the two lines to a third object or using a ruler.

2. Distribute centimeter rulers to students. Allow them to practice drawing lines of different lengths. Invite volunteers to share their measurements, and discuss how they used their rulers to accurately draw the lines.

Solve

1. Distribute copies of *Find the Lengths* to students. Have students work alone, in pairs, or in small groups.

2. Ask clarifying questions as students work, such as *How did you find this length? How did you know which one was longer?*

Debrief

1. What answers did you find? Explain your thinking.

2. Why is it important to look at the left side of the ruler as well as the right side?

Differentiate ◯

Some students may have difficulty remembering the measurements they have already found. Encourage students to record the measurements near the objects. If you wish to assign an exit card, consider the following task: *Draw three lines of different lengths. Label one* long, *one* longer, *and one* longest.

Draw an eraser above each ruler to show their lengths.

Margo's eraser is 10 cm long.

Bart's eraser is 5 cm long.

Maria's eraser is 7 cm long.

Write a sentence about the erasers using the word *longest*.

Draw a crayon above each ruler to show their lengths.

Zak's crayon is 6 cm long.

Caleb's crayon is 4 cm long.

Pam's crayon is 7 cm long.

Write two sentences about the crayons using the words *shorter* and *longest*.

Draw a pencil above each ruler to show their lengths.

Roberto's pencil is 8 cm long. Clara's pencil is 10 cm long. Pavel's pencil is 11 cm long. Kim Su's pencil is 13 cm long.

Write three sentences about the pencils using the words *shortest*, *longer*, and *longest*.

Lots of Ribbon

Standards
- Solves real-world problems involving addition and subtraction of whole numbers
- Understands the basic measure of length

Overview
Students solve problems involving length measures. They also write equations corresponding to the problems and use a variable to represent the unknown that they must find.

Problem-Solving Strategies
- Act it out or use manipulatives
- Count, compute, or write an equation
- Organize information in a picture, list, table, graph, or diagram

Materials
- *Lots of Ribbon* (page 95; lotsribbon.pdf)
- *Student Response Form* (page 130; studentresponse.pdf) *(optional)*

Activate
1. Display the following problem for students: *Brenda has a ribbon that is 24 inches long. She uses some of it to decorate a poster. Brenda has 16 inches of ribbon left. How many inches of ribbon did Brenda use on the poster?* Ask students what we might do to find this answer. Encourage a variety of responses. If not mentioned, ask *How might we use a yardstick to model this problem? What drawing could we make to help us? How would we write an equation to show this problem?*

2. Show students the equation $17 - \square = 12$. Tell students that you are going to start a story problem that matches this equation and that they will finish it. Tell students *I have 17 inches of velvet ribbon. I use some of it to ….* Have students share their ideas and then discuss how the problem matches the equation.

Solve
1. Distribute copies of *Lots of Ribbon* to students. Have students work alone, in pairs, or in small groups.

2. Ask refocusing questions as the students work, such as *What is the first piece of information you are given? How can you represent that information? What do you need to find?*

Debrief
1. What strategies did you use to find your answers? Show us your thinking.

2. How did you decide where to put the box when you wrote your equation?

3. How does writing equations help you solve problems?

Differentiate ⬤ ☆
Completing sentence frames such as the following may help students represent the problem with an equation: *I know... I need to find...*

Marcus has a red ribbon that is 32 inches long. It is 6 inches longer than his green ribbon. How long is the green ribbon?

Write an equation for this problem. Use ☐ for the number you need to find.

Marietta has a blue ribbon that is 23 inches long. She has a yellow ribbon that is longer. Placed end-to-end, the ribbons measure 50 inches. How long is the yellow ribbon?

Write an equation for this problem. Use ☐ for the number you need to find.

Janelle's mother gave her a piece of ribbon with red checks that was 79 inches long. She used 12 inches of the ribbon for her hair. She used 8 inches of the ribbon for a bookmark. She used the rest of the ribbon to wrap a gift. How long was the piece of ribbon Janelle used to wrap the gift?

Write an equation for this problem. Use ☐ for the number you need to find.

Finish the Story

Standard
Knows processes for measuring length using basic standard units

Overview
Students are given a story with missing information and a set of numbers, unit names, and measuring tool names to use to complete the story.

Problem-Solving Strategies

- Act it out or use manipulatives
- Guess and check or make an estimate
- Use logical reasoning

Materials

- *Finish the Story* (page 97; finishstory.pdf)
- rulers, yardsticks, and measuring tapes
- *Student Response Form* (page 130; studentresponse.pdf) *(optional)*

Activate

1. Ask students what tools they use to measure. Hold up a ruler, yardstick, or measuring tape when it is mentioned. If one of these tools is not mentioned, ask a question to trigger students' thinking. For example, ask *What might you use to measure your height?*

2. Record the names of these three tools and ask students to brainstorm different items they might measure with each one.

3. Ask questions to help students understand that each of the tools could be used to measure any of the lengths, but that some choices are better than others. For example, ask *Could I measure my height with a ruler? Which tool would be a better choice? Why?*

Solve

1. Distribute copies of *Finish the Story* to students. Have students work in pairs so that they can talk about their choices. Encourage students to read their complete stories aloud to make sure that they make sense.

2. Observe students as they work. Does each member of the pair contribute? How do they justify their thinking to one another? Do students refer to other known measures or situations to determine the best choices?

Debrief

1. How did you decide where to put the numbers? Did anyone use a different strategy?

2. What would you tell a friend who asked how to tell where the words should be placed?

Differentiate ○ ☆
Some students may need to have a ruler, yardstick, and measuring tape close by so that they can look at the tools as they make their choices. Other students may wish to act out the story using the tools.

Use each of the words and numbers in the box once to complete the story. The story must make sense.

inches	2	ruler	foot

Logan used a _____ to measure his pets. His parrot is

1 _____ tall. His guinea pig is 8 _____ long. His

dog is _____ feet long.

Use each of the words and numbers in the box once to complete the story. The story must make sense.

measuring tape	2	ruler	45	inches

Annie is in second grade. She is _____ inches tall. She

uses a _____ to find that the distance around her wrist is 6

_____. She uses a _____ to find that her pointer

finger is about _____ inches long.

Use each of the words and numbers in the box once to complete the story. The story must make sense.

yardstick	inches	30	feet	measuring tape

There is a firefighter and a fire hydrant in front of Marty's house. He
told her that he was 72 _____ tall and that a ladder on
his truck is 70 _____ long. Marty used a _____
to find the distance around the middle of the hydrant. She used a
_____ to measure the height of the hydrant. She found that

the hydrant is about _____ inches high.

Step-by-Step

Standards

- Counts whole numbers
- Makes organized lists of information necessary for solving a problem

Overview

Students determine the number of steps (heel-to-toe, walking, and giant) it takes to walk to different locations in the classroom. Then, they compare their results to determine which walk took a greater number of steps.

Problem-Solving Strategies

- Count, compute, or write an equation
- Organize information in a picture, list, table, graph, or diagram

Materials

- *Step-by-Step* (page 99; stepbystep.pdf)
- masking tape *(optional)*
- *Student Response Form* (page 130; studentresponse.pdf) *(optional)*

Activate

1. Ask students what they know about baby steps and giant steps. Have three volunteers model walking across the room. One student should take walking steps, one giant steps, and one should walk heel-to-toe. Have observing students describe each kind of step.

2. Have all students stand in a circle around the room. Call out a type of step and have students practice walking that way. Repeat until all steps have been practiced.

Solve

1. Distribute copies of *Step-by-Step* to students. Explain that they are to take walks and count the number of steps in each walk. Have students work in pairs so that one student can count the other student's steps.

2. As students work, ask them questions about their thinking, for example, *How do you keep track of the number of steps? How can you tell who has the longest walking-step?*

Debrief

1. How did having a chart help you to answer the questions?

2. Why might we get different answers when we walk somewhere from our desks?

3. Who thinks they took the greatest (or least) number of steps?

4. If you took two walks from your desk to the closest window and used baby steps one time and giant steps the next, which walk would take more steps? Why do you think so?

Differentiate ○ □ △ ☆

Students will be quite active when they are walking to collect their data and many of them will be moving in different directions. For students who find it difficult to focus in such an environment, consider allowing them to take walks in the hallway. Use masking tape to designate three distances for students to walk in place of those indicated in the problem.

Take giant steps. Record the number of steps.

Walk from your desk to:	Number of Giant Steps
the closest table	
the closest wall	
the closest door	

Did it take more steps to walk to the table or wall?

Take walking steps and giant steps. Record the number of steps.

Walk from your desk to:	Walking Steps	Giant Steps
the closest window		
the farthest table		
the farthest door		

Did it take more walking steps or giant steps to walk to the table? Why?

Take heel-to-toe steps and giant steps. Record the number of steps.

Walk from your desk to:	Heel-to-Toe Steps	Giant Steps
the teacher's desk		
the farthest window		
the farthest bookcase		

How many walking steps do you think it would take to walk to the window? Why do you think so?

Step-by-Step

Game Time

Standards

- Understands the concept of time and how it is measured
- Knows processes for telling time

Overview

Students are shown three analog clocks and given clues about the times of three children's games. Students match the times to the clocks and then record the time each clock shows.

Problem-Solving Strategies

- Act it out or use manipulatives
- Count, compute, or write an equation
- Find information in a picture, list, table, graph, or diagram
- Use logical reasoning

Materials

- *Game Time* (page 101; gametime.pdf)
- analog clocks (real or play)
- digital clocks *(optional)*
- *Student Response Form* (page 130; studentresponse.pdf) *(optional)*

Activate

1. Engage students in a conversation about the importance of schedules in sports. Ask questions such as *Do you play any team sports? How do you know when your team plays? What is a schedule? Why do you think games are scheduled at the beginning of a season for the whole season?*

2. Show students an analog clock set to 3:35. Ask *What time does this clock show? Is it a little before or a little after three-thirty? What time will it be one hour from now?*

Solve

1. Distribute copies of *Game Time* to students. Have students work alone, in pairs, or in small groups.

2. As students work, ask clarifying questions that will give you more access to students' thinking and help students to make their ideas more explicit. Ask *Why does it matter that all of the games start in the morning? Would it matter if one of the games was at night? How do you know which clock shows 11:35?*

Debrief

1. Which time did you identify first? Did anyone start with a different time?

2. How do you decide if one time is before or after another?

3. What is another name for eleven-thirty? Why do you think we sometimes use the phrase *half past* for this time?

Differentiate ○ □ △ ☆

Have students count aloud by fives as they touch each of the numerals on the clock face. To make the first problem more accessible to some students, you may want to show the times on digital clocks. Assign the exit-card task such as the following: *Draw a clock to show one-thirty.*

Write the name of the player under the clock that shows the starting time of the player's game.

Jacob has a soccer game at 10:15 A.M.

Lan has a soccer game at 11:30 A.M.

Pia has a soccer game at 10:20 A.M.

_____ _____ _____

Whose game starts first?

Write the name of the player under the clock that shows the starting time of the player's game. Write the time under each name.

Rick has a baseball game before Yuri does.

Quinn has a baseball game before 11:30 A.M.

_____ _____ _____

All of the games start in the morning.

_____ _____ _____

Draw hands on the clocks to show the time when each player's game begins. Write the name and time under each clock.

  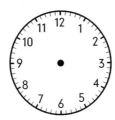

Jessie has a basketball game one hour after Owen.

Owen has a basketball game at 12:50.

Lanie has a basketball game at twenty-five minutes after three.

_____ _____ _____

All the games are in the afternoon.

_____ _____ _____

Tell a Story

Standards

- Understands the concept of time and how it is measured
- Knows processes for telling time

Overview

This problem set emphasizes the language of time. Students are provided with one or two pictures of clocks and two words. They use the words and time(s) in a story problem.

Problem-Solving Strategies

- Find information in a picture, list, table, graph, or diagram
- Use logical reasoning

Materials

- *Tell a Story* (page 103; tellstory.pdf)
- analog and digital clocks (real or play)
- *Student Response Form* (page 130; studentresponse.pdf) *(optional)*

Activate

1. Have students talk about the class's schedule for the day. Ask *What did we do first today? What time was that?* Write the time and the activities as the students mention them. Then, have each student work with a partner to create a story problem that uses this information. Encourage students to remember to ask a question in their stories. Provide time for several pairs to share their stories.

2. Tell students the following story: *Yesterday my friend and I agreed to walk together at six o'clock. We decided to meet at* (name a well-known place in the community). *I got up early and was there a few minutes before six. I stretched as I waited for my friend, but she never showed up. I tried to reach her on the phone, but there was no answer. I was busy after school and didn't check my phone messages until six-thirty. My friend had called and said, "Hi, it's six o'clock. Where are you?"* Ask students what they think happened.

3. Have students brainstorm until someone suggests that you were there at six in the morning and your friend was there at six in the evening. Ask students what we write after times so that everyone knows whether we mean in the morning or in the evening. (A.M. *or* P.M.)

Solve

1. Distribute copies of *Tell a Story* to students. Have students work in pairs or in small groups.

2. Ask questions to engage students, such as *What would you want to happen first?*

Debrief

1. What problems did you write?

2. How are your problems alike and different?

Differentiate ○ □ △ ☆

Pair or group students so that each team has members who are capable story writers.

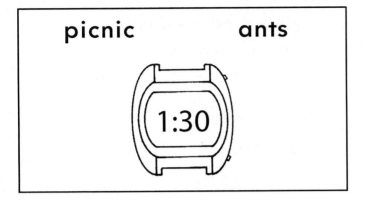

Write a story problem. Use each word and the time in the box. Be sure to write A.M. or P.M. so the story makes sense.

Write a story problem. Use each word and time in the box. Be sure to write A.M. or P.M. so the story makes sense.

Write a story problem. Use each word and time in the box. Be sure to use A.M. and P.M. so the story makes sense.

Leo's Days

Standards

- Understands the concept of time and how it is measured
- Knows processes for telling time

Overview

Students match events to the times shown on analog or digital clocks. Clues about the times include showing the written time or phrases such as *just before 4:00.*

Problem-Solving Strategies

- Count, compute, or write an equation
- Find information in a picture, list, table, graph, or diagram
- Use logical reasoning

Materials

- *Leo's Days* (page 105; leosdays.pdf)
- *Rosie's Times* (rosiestimes.pdf)
- analog and digital clocks (real or play)
- *Student Response Form* (page 130; studentresponse.pdf) *(optional)*

Activate

1. Display or distribute copies of *Rosie's Times.* Read the clues aloud to students or have students volunteer to read them aloud to the class. Have students talk with a partner about which clock times match each activity. Have students share their thinking. Encourage students to justify their thinking by asking questions such as *How did you know that clock was the correct choice?*

2. Review the use of A.M. and P.M. and have students write the times for each clock, given the clues.

3. If your schedule allows, you may want to ask students about special times in their days.

Solve

1. Distribute copies of *Leo's Days* to students. Have students work alone, in pairs, or in small groups.

2. Make clocks available for students to use. Some students may want to move the clocks to see the time that is one or two hours later or to prove to themselves that a time such as 3:55 is close to 4:00.

Debrief

1. How did you decide on the answers? Did anyone think differently?

2. What might you think about when we draw hands to show a time?

3. Do you find one type of clock easier to use than another? Why or why not?

Differentiate ⚫ ◼

Students find it easier to realize that 2:55 is almost 3:00 on an analog clock than on a digital one, so make sure both are available. You may want some students to explore a clock that only has an hour hand. Direct students to notice the hand at various intervals within an hour. Ask *Do you think it is closer to 2:00 or 3:00? How do you know? Where do you think the hour hand will be when it is 2:30?*

Use the times on the clocks to fill in the blanks in the story. Write A.M. or P.M. after each time. Be sure your story makes sense.

On Friday Leo has lunch

at _____. He gets out of

school at _____. He gets

home at _____.

Use the times on the clocks to fill in the blanks in the story. Write A.M. or P.M. after each time. Be sure your story makes sense.

On Saturday Leo gets up at _____.

His older sister gets up two hours later

at _____. After lunch Leo takes

his dog for a long walk and gets home

at _____. He has a swim lesson at

three o'clock. Leo gets home just before

4:00, at _____.

Use the times on the clocks to fill in the blanks in the story. Write A.M. or P.M. after each time. Be sure your story makes sense.

On Sunday Leo gets up at _____.
His family has lunch just before noon, at
_____. At two o'clock they all
drive to his grandma's house and get
there at _____.

An hour later at _____ he helps
his grandma make dinner. The family gets
home at seven-thirty. Leo gets ready for
bed and is asleep by _____.

Coin Combos

Standard

Knows processes for counting money

Overview

In this problem set, students are given the total amount of money and asked to identify the coins in the collection.

Problem-Solving Strategies

- Act it out or use manipulatives
- Count, compute, or write an equation
- Find information in a picture, list, table, graph, or diagram
- Guess and check or make an estimate

Materials

- *Coin Combos* (page 107; coincombos.pdf)
- one real penny, nickel, dime, and quarter
- U.S. coins (real or play)
- *Student Response Form* (page 130; studentresponse.pdf) *(optional)*

Activate

1. Ask a volunteer to come to the front of the room. Have the student close his or her eyes and then place a coin in the volunteer's hand. Have the student try to identify the name of the coin without looking at it.

2. Repeat step 1 with different volunteers and coins until each of the four coins have been identified. If extra coins and time are available, have students repeat this activity in pairs.

3. Write the names of the coins on the board. Ask students to identify the value of each coin. Record the value beside each coin's name.

4. Draw four circles on the board and write the value 17¢. Explain that the circles indicate the number of coins that total 17¢, but not their size. Have students work in pairs to decide on the names of the coins. (*one dime, one nickel, and two pennies*)

Solve

1. Distribute copies of *Coin Combos* to students. Have students work alone, in pairs, or in small groups.

2. As students work, note who makes and checks several guesses, who appears to compute mentally, and who uses coins to model the problems.

Debrief

1. What are the coins? How did you decide?

2. Does anyone have a different solution to share?

Differentiate ☆

Some students may not be familiar with U.S. coins. Review the coins with these students before the lesson begins and provide them with a list of the coins and their values.

Which coins are in the jar?

There are _____ dimes,

_____ nickels, and

_____ penny in the jar.

Manny has seven coins.

He has 40¢.

He has no nickels.

What coins does Manny have?

Aubrey has 30¢.

She has at least one penny, one nickel, and one dime.

What coins could she have?

Find three possible answers.

Joke Sale

Standard
Knows processes for counting money

Overview
In this problem set, students are shown a collection of money and one or two items for sale. They identify the coins they need to use or write the amount of money they have left after a purchase.

Problem-Solving Strategies
- Act it out or use manipulatives
- Count, compute, or write an equation
- Find information in a picture, list, table, graph, or diagram

Materials
- *Joke Sale* (page 109; jokesale.pdf)
- U.S. coins (real or play)
- *Student Response Form* (page 130; studentresponse.pdf) *(optional)*

Activate
1. Display a quarter, a dime, a nickel, and a penny for students. Ask a volunteer to make 15¢ from this collection. Repeat this activity with other possible totals.

2. Show another collection, for example one quarter, two dimes, one nickel, and four pennies. This time, have students take turns providing both the total values and the answers.

Solve
1. Distribute copies of *Joke Sale* to students. Have students work alone, in pairs, or in small groups.

2. Encourage students by giving them descriptive feedback as they work, for example *I see you recorded the amount of money that is shown. I see you are crossing out coins that are not needed to pay.*

Debrief
1. How did you find the answer?

2. How do you find the value of a collection of coins?

3. Does anyone find the value of a collection of coins a different way?

Differentiate ● ☆
Some students may prefer to act out the problem using coins. Have them pretend they are in a joke store, pay the amount indicated on the price tag, and then find the value of the coins that are left. You may wish to consider providing an exit-card task, such as the following: *You have five dimes. You buy something for 39¢. How much money do you have left?*

I had

I bought a rubber spider.

Circle the coins I have left.

I had

I bought a rubber snake.

Write how much money I have now.

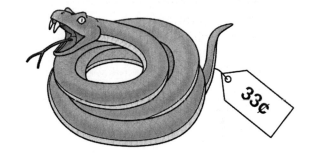

I had

I bought a rubber chicken and a rubber mouse.

Write how much money I have now.

All My Coins

Standards

- Counts whole numbers
- Solves real-world problems involving addition and subtraction of whole numbers
- Knows processes for counting money
- Collects and represents information about objects or events in simple graphs

Overview

Students are given a graph that shows the number of quarters, dimes, nickels, and pennies someone has. They find the information in the graph to answer questions about amounts of money that involve finding totals and differences.

Problem-Solving Strategies

- Count, compute, or write an equation
- Find information in a picture, list, table, graph, or diagram
- Guess and check or make an estimate

Materials

- *All My Coins* (page 111; allmycoins.pdf)
- *Coin Bar Graph* (coingraph.pdf)
- U.S. coins (real or play)
- *Student Response Form* (page 130; studentresponse.pdf) *(optional)*

Activate

1. Display a collection of coins for students. Ask them what they can tell you about these coins. Then, ask them how they might group the coins to make them easier to count. Invite a student to sort the coins according to their values.

2. Display *Coin Bar Graph* and have volunteers make a bar for the coins in each set.

3. Ask students if there are more nickels or dimes. Ask *If I were going to give you some coins, would you rather have these dimes or these nickels? Why?*

Solve

1. Distribute copies of *All My Coins* to students and provide coins for students to use. Have students work alone, in pairs, or in small groups.

2. As students work, ask refocusing and clarifying questions, such as *How could counting by tens help you? What coins are you using when you count by five?*

Debrief

1. Who can show us how to find the answer?

2. How else could we find the answer?

Differentiate

To provide more practice with graphs and money, give groups of two to four students a collection of coins and a copy of the *Coin Bar Graph*. Have students make a graph to show the number of coins. Then, have them write the total value of the coins.

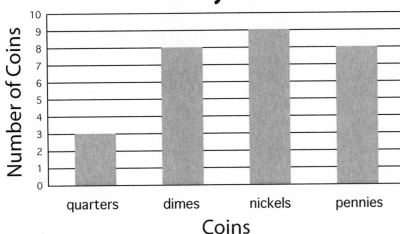

All My Coins

What is the total value of my dimes?

I use my dimes to buy a drink for 79¢. What coin is my change?

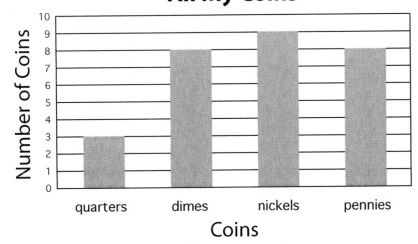

All My Coins

Together, how much are my nickels and pennies worth?

I use these coins to buy a snack for 40¢. What nickels and pennies could I have left? Find two ways.

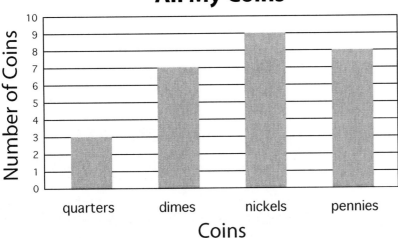

All My Coins

I buy a bottle of orange juice with all my quarters and dimes. I use all my nickels and pennies to buy an apple. How much more does the orange juice cost than the apple?

Money Matters

Standards

- Knows processes for counting money
- Solves real-world problems involving addition and subtraction

Overview

Students are shown a collection of money which includes dollar bills and coins. Students then compare the total to a greater value, compare it to the value of another collection, or determine the coins added when a value increases.

Problem-Solving Strategies

- Act it out or use manipulatives
- Count, compute, or write an equation
- Find information in a picture, list, table, graph, or diagram

Materials

- *Money Matters* (page 113; moneymatters.pdf)
- U.S. coins and dollar bills (real or play)
- *Student Response Form* (page 130; studentresponse.pdf) *(optional)*

Activate

1. If students are not familiar with the dollar bill, provide some time for them to look at one. Have them talk about what they see on the bill. Ask them how we might remember that President Washington is on the one dollar bill.

2. Show students two collections of money, both involving bills and coins. Review the correct way to record these amounts of money.

3. Ask students which collection has a greater value. Ask *What can you do to prove that to us? Does anyone know another way?*

4. Repeat steps 2 and 3 with different collections of money.

Solve

1. Distribute copies of *Money Matters* to students. Have students work alone, in pairs, or in small groups.

2. Have money available for students to use. Using coins may be particularly helpful for solving these problems. This is a good opportunity for students to recognize that using manipulatives can be helpful at all levels of challenge.

Debrief

1. How did you find the amount of money? Did anyone find it a different way?

2. How might you think differently if the amount of money was listed but there was no picture?

Differentiate ⬤

Some students have difficulty remembering how to record the value of money using a dollar sign and decimal point. Some students may write a cent sign after the total, while others may use all three signs. Provide a graphic organizer with one column before a decimal point and two columns after.

Gabby needs $4.50 to buy her friend a puzzle. How much more money does Gabby need?

Who has more money, Luke or Stephan?

How much more?

Soledad's sister gives her 5 more coins.

Now Soledad has $6.20.

How much money did Soledad's sister give her?

What coins did Soledad get?

What Shape Is Next?

Standards
- Uses the names of simple geometric shapes to represent and describe real-world situations
- Extends simple patterns

Overview
Students recognize and create geometric patterns.

Problem-Solving Strategies
- Act it out or use manipulatives
- Generalize a pattern

Materials
- *What Shape Is Next?* (page 115; whatshapenext.pdf)
- pattern blocks
- *Student Response Form* (page 130; studentresponse.pdf) *(optional)*

Activate
1. Distribute pattern blocks to students. If they have not used the materials recently, provide some time for free exploration and review the names of the shapes. Identify all of the shapes with four sides (the square and rhombuses) as *quadrilaterals*.

2. Have students make a row of blocks in this order: hexagon, triangle, rhombus, hexagon, triangle, rhombus, hexagon. Ask students what shape will come next. (*triangle*) Ask them what the unit is that repeats. (*hexagon, triangle, rhombus*)

3. Repeat step 2 with the following sequence: hexagon, triangle, triangle, hexagon, triangle, triangle, hexagon. (triangle; hexagon, triangle, triangle)

Solve
1. Distribute copies of *What Shape Is Next?* to students. Leave the blocks available for those students who would benefit from building the patterns to better understand them. Have students work alone or in pairs, or students could build the pattern in a small group and then each make their own decision about which shape is next.

2. As students work, ask them why they have decided on certain shapes to continue the pattern. Also ask them to identify the repeating unit.

3. Invite students to place their drawings on their desks and take a gallery walk to see the patterns made by different students. Encourage them to travel in pairs and talk about the shape they think will be next.

Debrief
1. What shape do you think comes next? What could you say to convince someone that your choice makes sense?

2. What did you notice about the patterns your classmates made? What made some of them more (less) challenging?

Differentiate ⬤ ◼ △ ☆
If possible, make pattern block cutouts or tracing templates available for students who may struggle with drawing the shapes.

Draw the next shape in the pattern.

Write the name of the shape you drew.

Draw a different pattern using triangles and quadrilaterals.

Write the name of the next shape.

Draw a different pattern using hexagons and quadrilaterals.

Write the name of the next shape.

Draw a different pattern using hexagons, quadrilaterals, and triangles.

What Shape Am I?

Standards

- Understands basic properties of simple geometric shapes and similarities and differences between simple geometric shapes
- Uses the names of simple geometric shapes to represent and describe real-world situations

Overview

In this problem set, students are given pictures of shapes and some clues. Students use the clues to identify one of the shapes.

Problem-Solving Strategy

Use logical reasoning

Materials

- *What Shape Am I?* (page 117; whatshape.pdf)
- *Student Response Form* (page 130; studentresponse.pdf) *(optional)*

Activate

1. Draw a picture of a triangle, quadrilateral, pentagon, and hexagon and review the names of the shapes.

2. Tell students that you are thinking of one of these shapes and that you will give them clues to help them find it. Say *My shape has more than three sides.* Have students tell what they know about your shape from the clue. Model crossing off the triangle to show that it is no longer a possibility. Then, say *My shape has fewer than five angles.* Again, have students tell you what they know and model crossing off the pentagon and the hexagon. Emphasize the importance of checking their thinking. Say *Let's check the quadrilateral with the two clues. Does it have more than three sides? Does it have fewer than five angles?*

Solve

1. Distribute copies of *What Shape Am I?* to students. Have students work alone or in pairs.

2. To familiarize students with polygons in nontraditional positions, point to the triangle and ask students to name the shape.

Debrief

1. Which shape did you identify?

2. How did you keep track of what you learned from the clues?

3. How did you check your work?

Differentiate ⬤ ☆

Some students may need to refer to a vocabulary list. If not already available, have a small group of students create entries for a word wall or make a geometric reference sheet for their journals. For each term have students write a definition and provide drawings. Make sure drawings show a variety of possible shapes. For example, all of the triangles should not have three equal sides or be right triangles.

I am not a square.

I have only three angles.

I am a _____.

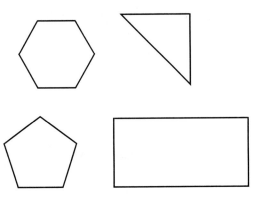

I have fewer than
five angles.

I am not a triangle.

I am a _____.

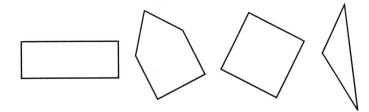

I have more than
three angles.

I am not a quadrilateral.

I am a _____.

Triangles and Squares

Standards

- Adds and subtracts whole numbers
- Uses the names of simple geometric shapes to represent and describe real-world situations
- Extends simple patterns

Overview

In this problem set, students are shown designs made with triangles and squares. Students find patterns among the given examples and use the generalizations, along with counting or computation skills, to predict the number of triangles and squares in a later iteration of the pattern.

Problem-Solving Strategies

- Act it out or use manipulatives
- Count, compute, or write an equation
- Generalize a pattern
- Organize information in a picture, list, table, graph, or diagram

Materials

- *Triangles and Squares* (page 119; trianglessquares.pdf)
- pattern blocks
- *Student Response Form* (page 130; studentresponse.pdf) *(optional)*

Activate

1. Sketch the following pattern of brick walls for students:

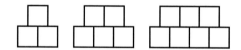

   Ask students to describe what they see. Encourage several responses.

2. Ask students how the next brick wall will look. Draw the next brick wall according to students' directions and have them tell you how they know it fits the pattern.

3. Ask students how they could find the total number of squares. Ask them to share other ways to find the total.

Solve

1. Distribute copies of *Triangles and Squares* to students. Have students work alone, in pairs, or in small groups. Have pattern blocks available for students who wish to build the designs.

2. As students work, observe how they find the total numbers. Do they count, use mental arithmetic, or write equations?

Debrief

1. What patterns did you see?

2. How did you find the total numbers? What would be another way to find them?

Differentiate △

Students ready for a greater challenge may wish to make their own pattern problems and share them with classmates.

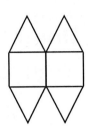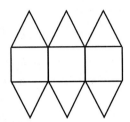

The pattern continues.

If there are 4 squares, how many triangles will there be?

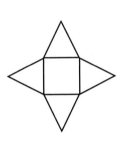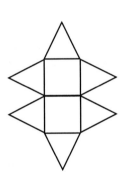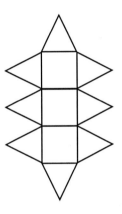

The pattern continues.

If there are 7 squares, how many triangles will there be?

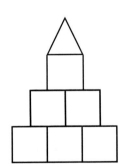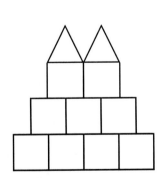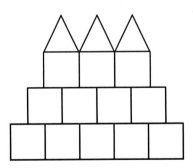

The pattern continues.

If there are 21 squares, how many triangles will there be?

Dot Squares

Standard

Understands the concept of a unit and its subdivision into equal parts

Overview

In this problem set, students are shown a figure on an array of dots. They connect the dots to find the total number of small squares they can make within the figure.

Problem-Solving Strategy

Find information in a picture, list, table, graph, or diagram

Materials

- *Dot Squares* (page 121; dotsquares.pdf)
- *Dot Paper Template* (dotpaper.pdf)
- geoboards and elastic bands (*optional*)
- *Student Response Form* (page 130; studentresponse.pdf) (*optional*)

Activate

1. Begin with a game of dots to engage students in these problems. Mark off a five by five dot area on the *Dot Paper Template* for the game board. Players alternate turns, making a line segment from any dot to any adjacent dot. (Diagonal line segments are not allowed.) The player who makes a line segment that forms a small square claims the square by initialing the square, then that player gets another turn. The game ends when no further segments can be drawn. Play a class game in teams to review the game. If time allows, have students play again in pairs.

2. Mark off an array of three dots by four dots. Ask, *If you were playing dots and every small square was made on this board, how many small squares would there be?* (6)

Solve

1. Distribute copies of *Dot Squares* to students. Have students work alone or in pairs.

2. Provide reinforcing feedback as students work, such as *I see that you are drawing your lines carefully to make sure you make all of the squares.*

Debrief

1. How did you find the number of squares? Show us.

2. Did anyone find the answer another way?

3. I heard someone say 9 + 3 + 1 = 13 to solve the second problem. Why do you think these numbers were used? How might you use an equation to represent one of the other problems?

Differentiate

Some students may wish to use geoboards and elastic bands to mark the squares.

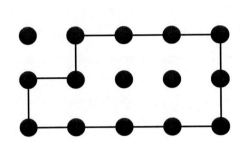

 = 1 small square

Connect the dots to show all the small squares inside the figure.

How many small squares are there?

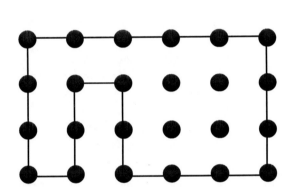

 = 1 small square

Connect the dots to show all the small squares inside the figure.

How many small squares are there?

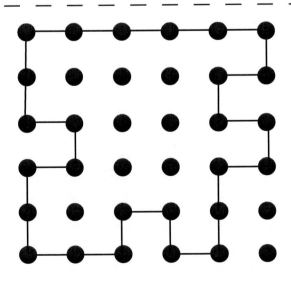

 = 1 small square

Connect the dots to show all of the small squares inside the figure.

How many small squares are there?

Shape Symbols

Standards

- Understands the concept of a unit and its subdivision into equal parts
- Understands basic properties of simple geometric shapes and similarities and differences between simple geometric shapes

Overview

Students are shown examples of symbols that do and do not fit a category. Students must decide which of three given symbols meet the conditions to be included in the category.

Problem-Solving Strategies

- Find information in a picture, list, table, graph, or diagram
- Generalize a pattern
- Use logical reasoning

Materials

- *Shape Symbols* (page 123; shapesymbols.pdf)
- *Student Response Form* (page 130; studentresponse.pdf) *(optional)*

Activate

1. Show four figures such as the ones below and tell students that the ones on the left are "circs" and the ones on the right are not "circs."

   These are circs.   These are not circs.

   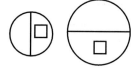

2. Ask students how they would describe a circ. (*A circle cut in half with a square drawn in one half.*). Ask a volunteer to draw a new one for the class.

Solve

1. Distribute copies of *Shape Symbols* to students. Tell students that the figures on the left fit the rules, while those on the right do not. Make sure students understand that they are to use this information to decide which one of the following figures also fits the category. Have students work alone, in pairs, or in small groups.

2. As students work you may wish to note how they discuss the features of the shapes. Do they refer to equal parts or mention halves, thirds, or fourths?

Debrief

1. How would you describe a (name of category)?

2. How did you decide which figure fit the group?

3. What figure could you draw that would also fit?

Differentiate

Students who are not strong visual learners may be challenged by the way the information is presented. Have them describe what they see to a partner. The words will help them identify common attributes.

These are all haps.

None of these are haps.

Which shape below is a hap?

A   B   C

These are all thaps.

None of these are thaps.

Which shape below is a thap?

A   B   C

These are all fops.

None of these are fops.

Which shape below is a fop?

A   B   C

How Many Cubes?

Standards

- Understands basic properties of simple geometric shapes and similarities and differences between simple geometric shapes
- Uses the names of simple geometric shapes to represent and describe real-world situations

Overview

Students are shown figures composed of cubes, some of which are hidden. Their task is to determine the total number of cubes in the figure.

Problem-Solving Strategies

- Act it out or use manipulatives
- Count, compute, or write an equation
- Find information in a picture, list, table, graph, or diagram
- Use logical reasoning

Materials

- *How Many Cubes?* (page 125; howmanycubes.pdf)
- *Building Blocks* (buildingblocks.pdf)
- small cubes
- *Student Response Form* (page 130; studentresponse.pdf) (*optional*)

Activate

1. Hold up a cube and ask students to name the shape. Ask them how they know it is a cube.

2. Display *Building Blocks* and ask students to determine the number of cubes it would take to build this figure.

3. Ask students for their answers. If there is disagreement, have them explain their thinking. If students all agree, ask *What would you tell someone who thought there were only four cubes?*

Solve

1. Distribute copies of *How Many Cubes?* to students. Have small cubes available for students to use to build the figures if they choose to do so. Have students work alone, in pairs, or in small groups.

2. Ask refocusing and clarifying questions, such as *How many cubes do you think are in the bottom row? What would happen if there were not a cube underneath this one?*

Debrief

1. How many cubes do you think are needed? Why do you think so?

2. How are these buildings alike or different?

3. How might the answer to one of these problems help you to answer another one?

4. What would you tell others to think about when they try to find the number of cubes?

Differentiate ○ □ △ ☆

Visual problems provide an opportunity for different students to share their strengths. It is important for these students to recognize that their skills are relevant to mathematics. To challenge students, have them try to draw the figures shown or draw their own building problems to share.

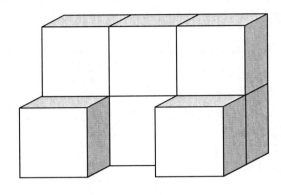

How many cubes does it take to build this figure?

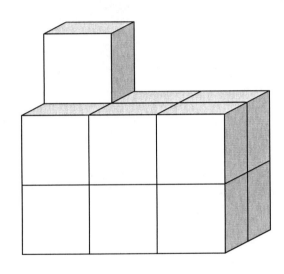

How many cubes does it take to build this figure?

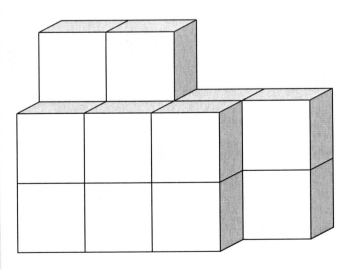

How many cubes does it take to build this figure?

Make the Whole

Standard

Understands the concept of a unit and its subdivision into equal parts

Overview

In this problem set, students are shown a picture of a fractional part and asked to draw a picture of the whole.

Problem-Solving Strategies

- Find information in a picture, list, table, graph, or diagram
- Guess and check or make an estimate
- Organize information in a picture, list, table, graph, or diagram

Materials

- *Make the Whole* (page 127; makewhole.pdf)
- scissors
- *Student Response Form* (page 130; studentresponse.pdf) *(optional)*

Activate

1. Ask students what one-fourth means. Allow for a variety of responses. Ask *If you shared a cookie with three friends and each of you ate the same amount, how much did each of you eat? If you each ate different amounts, would the parts you ate still be one-fourth because there were four of you?*

2. Draw a half-circle and say *Imagine you ate half of a cookie and this is the piece you ate. Who thinks they can draw the whole cookie? Why do you think the whole looks like this?*

Solve

1. Distribute copies of *Make the Whole* to students. Have students work in pairs or in small groups and tell them to explain their thinking to each other.

2. Ask clarifying and refocusing questions as students work, such as *How many pieces of this size were there in the whole? Is there another way to draw the whole?*

Debrief

1. How do you think the whole looked? Why do you think so?

2. Could it look another way?

3. What do you notice about the wholes for these problems? Why do you think this happens?

Differentiate

Some students may wish to cut out the fractional piece and use it to create the whole. Have scissors available for those who wish to use them.

Mac ate half of a cracker.

Here is the piece he ate.

What did the cracker look like before Mac ate half of it?

Draw to show the whole.

Naomi ate one-fourth of a sandwich.

Here is the piece she ate.

What did the sandwich look like before Naomi ate one-fourth of it?

Draw to show the whole.

Pedro ate one-fourth of a pizza.

Here is the piece he ate.

What did the pizza look like before Pedro ate one-fourth of it?

Draw to show the whole.

Find the Triangles

Standards

- Uses the names of simple geometric shapes to represent and describe real-world situations
- Understands that patterns can be made by putting different shapes together or taking them apart

Overview

Students are shown a geometric figure and asked to count the number of triangles they can find in the figure.

Problem-Solving Strategies

- Find information in a picture, list, table, graph, or diagram
- Organize information in a picture, list, table, graph, or diagram

Materials

- *Find the Triangles* (page 129; findtriangles.pdf)
- *Student Response Form* (page 130; studentresponse.pdf) *(optional)*

Activate

1. Sketch the figure below for students and ask them how many triangles they see.

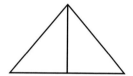

2. Many students may suggest that there are two triangles. If a student does not suggest that there are three triangles, ask *What do you see when you outline the whole shape?*

Solve

1. Distribute copies of *Find the Triangles* to students. Have students work alone or in pairs.

2. As students work, provide reinforcing feedback, such as *I see that you are looking carefully to find all of the triangles.*

Debrief

1. How many triangles did you find? Does anyone have a different answer?

2. What did you do to make sure you found them all?

3. How might you convince your classmates that you found them all?

Differentiate ⬤ ▢ △ ☆

Show students a way to organize their thinking by labeling each region in the figure with a letter. Then, students can make a list of the triangles by writing the letters. For example: A, B, and AB.

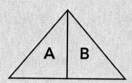

How many triangles are there in this figure?

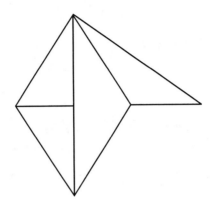

How many triangles are there in this figure?

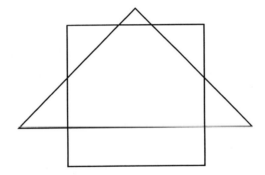

How many triangles are there in this figure?

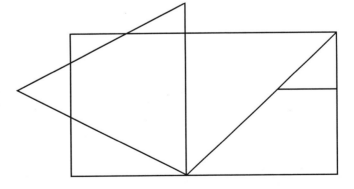

#50774—50 Leveled Math Prob

Name: _____   Date: _____

Student Response Form

Problem:

(glue your problem here)

My Work and Illustrations:
(picture, table, list, graph)

My Solution:

My Explanation:

_____

_____

Individual Observation Form

Name: _____ Date: _____

Shows Understanding (Check all that apply.)

☐ Makes representations or notes to understand more fully.

☐ Talks with a peer to understand more fully.

☐ Asks teacher questions to understand more fully.

☐ Interprets problem correctly.

Applies Strategies (Check all that apply.)

☐ Demonstrates use of an appropriate strategy.

☐ Tries an alternative approach when first attempt is unsuccessful.

☐ Uses a strategy appropriately after it is suggested by someone else.

Explains or Justifies Thinking (Check all that apply.)

☐ Communicates thinking clearly.

☐ Uses words and labels to summarize steps to solution.

☐ Provides mathematical justifications for solution or solution process.

☐ Uses correct mathematical vocabulary.

Takes It Further (Check all that apply.)

☐ Makes connections among problems.

☐ Poses new related problems.

☐ Solves a problem in more than one way.

Group Observation Form

Use this form to record scores, comments, or both.

Date: _____

Scores: 1—Beginning 2—Developing 3—Meeting 4—Exceeding											
Group Members	Provides leadership/ suggestions to group	Builds on the comments of others	Communicates clearly, uses correct mathematical vocabulary, and builds on the ideas of others	Creates at least one accurate representation of the problem	Suggests/ chooses appropriate strategies						

Record-Keeping Chart

Use this chart to record the problems that were completed. Record the name of the lesson and the date when the appropriate level was completed.

Name: _____

Lesson	⬤ Date Completed	⬛ Date Completed	▲ Date Completed

Answer Key

Who Is Who? (page 31)

- ● Mia: 2; Jake: 11; Lucy: 7; Rick: 6
- ■ Carla: 14; Will: 9; Mandy: 3; Pablo: 8
- ▲ Cal: 9; Eliza: 15; Rudo: 7; Andi: 11

Design Blocks (page 33)

- ● 6 squares
- ■ 7 triangles
- ▲ James 1, Henry 14; James 2, Henry 13; James 3, Henry 12; James 4, Henry 11; James 5, Henry 10; James 6, Henry 9; James 7, Henry 8

Yard Sale (page 35)

(Note that any symbol may be used for the unknown number and equations may vary.)

- ● $11.00; $8.00 + $3.00 = ?
- ■ $12.00; $2.00 + ? = $14.00
- ▲ $3.00; $9.00 + ? + ? = $15.00

Equal Sums (page 37)

- ● move the 1 from Box 2 to Box 4
- ■ move the 4 from Box 3 to Box 4
- ▲ move the 6 from the Box 4 to Box 1

Venn Diagrams (page 39)

●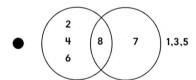

■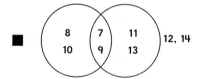

- ▲ Less Than 10; Even Numbers

Books for Sale (page 41)

- ● *Rocks* and *Sports*
- ■ *Frogs* and *Plants* or *Jokes* and *Plants*
- ▲ *Baseball*, *Space*, and *China*

Rubber Band Shapes (page 43)

- ● 23: How many animal bands do Emily and Nigel have together?

  7: How many fewer animal bands does Nigel have than Emily? Or, How many more animal bands does Emily have than Nigel?

- ■ 36: How many animal bands do Wendell and Pablo have together?

  16: How many more animal bands does Pablo have than Wendell? Or, How many fewer animal bands does Wendell have than Pablo?

  7: How many more people bands does Wendell have than animal bands? Or, How many fewer animal bands does Wendell have than people bands?

- ▲ 60: How many bands does Li Ming have in all?

  30: How many more people bands than animal bands does Tala have? Or, How many fewer animal bands does Tala have than people brands?

  26: How many more animal bands does Li Ming have than Tala? Or, How many fewer animal bands does Tala have than Li Ming?

  6: How many more bands does Tala have than Li Ming? Or, How many fewer bands does Li Ming have than Tala?

Make a Face (page 45)

- ● 24 points
- ■ 7 points
- ▲ Drawings will vary. Possible solution: two identical faces, but one with glasses and mustache.

Field Day (page 47)

- ● 65 points
- ■ 56 children; 68 children
- ▲ 100 children

Answer Key *(cont.)*

Pose a Problem (page 49)

- $25 + 5 = ?$ or a related subtraction equation; problems will vary; 30
- ■ $32 + ? = 53$ or a related addition or subtraction equation; problems will vary; 21
- ▲ $? + 27 = 92$ or a related addition or subtraction equation; problems will vary; 65

Bagfuls (page 51)

- 9 cookies
- ■ 16 pieces of fruit
- ▲ 30 muffins

Salad Garden (page 53)

- 10 tomato plants; drawings will be in groups of 2 or 5
- ■ 12 lettuce plants; possible equations include $4 + 4 + 4 = 12$ and $3 + 3 + 3 + 3 = 12$
- ▲ 15 carrots; possible equations include $5 + 5 + 5 = 15$ and $3 + 3 + 3 + 3 + 3 = 15$

What Am I Thinking? (page 55)

- 7 and 5
- ■ 15 and 5
- ▲ 22 and 8

Same Sums (page 57)

(Arrangement within a line may vary.)

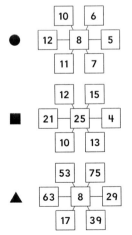

Puzzlers (page 59)

- 20; choice will vary; 20; reasons will vary but should include reference to seven being added and then subtracted
- ■ 41; choice will vary; 41; reasons will vary but should include reference to the subtraction of 19 and 2 being balanced by the addition of 21
- ▲ 65; choice will vary; 65; reasons will vary but should include reference to the addition of 15 and 17 (total of 32) being balanced by subtracting 29 and 3 (also a total of 32)

Animal Stories (page 61)

- Answers will vary, but $B + C + D = A$
- ■ Answers will vary, but $B + D = C$ and $C + D + E = A$
- ▲ Answers will vary, but $B + C = D$ and $B + D + E + F = A$

Number Blocks (page 63)

- 252
- ■ 267; 2 hundreds, 1 ten, and 2 ones
- ▲ 3 hundreds

Figure It (page 65)

- ⊗ = 6   and   △ = 31
- ■ ◯ = 2   and   ☆ = 129
- ▲ ✕ = 58   and   ☺ = 42

Predict the Number (page 67)

- 47; Questions will vary.
- ■ 69; Questions will vary.
- ▲ 640; Questions will vary.

Answer Key *(cont.)*

Living on Main Street (page 69)

● 135

■ 257

▲ 538

Machine Math (page 71)

● A = 25; B = 33; It subtracts 22, or
In − 22 = Out

■ A = 46; B = 120; It subtracts 17, or
In − 17 = Out

▲ A = 220; B = 49; It subtracts 84, or
In − 84 = Out

Show It (page 73)

● Answers will vary; possibilities include: 111,
112, 113, 114, and 115

■ Answers will vary; possibilities include: 121,
122, 131, 132, 141, 142, 231, 232, 241, 242

▲ Answers will vary; possibilities include: 121,
131, 132, 141, 142, 143, 221, 231, 232, 241,
242, 243

Where Is It? (page 75)

● 30; 40

■ 210; 310

▲ 260; 370

Finish the Equations (page 77)

● 37 = 30 + 7 or 37 = 7 + 30; 15 − 2 = 13

■ 82 = 34 + 48 or 82 = 48 + 34; 125 − 119 = 6;
10 + 4 = 14 or 4 + 10 = 14

▲ 283 = 147 + 136 or 283 = 136 + 147;
147 − 31 = 116; 257 − 136 = 121 or
257 − 121 = 136

Ring Toss (page 79)

● 131 points; 141 points

■ 327 points

▲ 392, 401, or 491 points

Counting Along (page 81)

● 2, 4, 6, 8, 10, predictions and reasons will
vary; 10

■ 10, 20, 30, 40, 50, 60, 70, 80, 90, 100;
predictions and reasons will vary; 30;

▲ 5, 10, 15, 20, 25, 30, 35, 40, 45, 50;
predictions and reasons will vary; 80

The Lee Family (page 83)

● 132; 14; 11; 16

■ 8; 142; 99; 100; 5

▲ 850; 100; 950; 5; 50; 54

From the Beginning (page 85)

● 125

■ 175

▲ 280

All About Us (page 87)

● 7 children

■ 15 children

▲ 23 children

Last Names (page 89)

Answers will vary.

Measure It (page 91)

Answers will vary.

Find the Lengths (page 93)

● Lines drawn should show 10 cm, 5 cm, and
7 cm; Margo's eraser is longest.

■ Lines drawn should show 6 cm, 4 cm, 7
cm; Zak's (or Caleb's) pencil is shorter than
Pam's; Pam's crayon is longest.

▲ Lines drawn should show 8 cm, 10 cm,
11 cm, and 13 cm; Roberto's pencil is
shortest; Clara's (Pavel's/Kim Su's) pencil
is longer than Roberto's; Kim Su's pencil is
longest.

Answer Key *(cont.)*

Lots of Ribbon (page 95)

● 26 in.; $32 - 6 = \square$ or $6 + \square = 32$

■ 27 in.; $23 + \square = 50$ or $50 - 23 = \square$

▲ 59 in.; $12 + 8 + \square = 79$ or
$79 - 12 - 8 = \square$

Finish the Story (page 97)

● ruler; foot; inches; 2;

■ 45; measuring tape; inches; ruler; 2

▲ inches; feet; measuring tape; yardstick; 30

Step-by-Step (page 99)

● Answers will vary.

■ Answers will vary, but the number of walking steps should be greater than the number of giant steps and the explanation should refer to the fact that giant steps are longer than walking steps, so fewer are needed (or the reverse).

▲ Answers will vary but the number of walking steps should be between that of heel-to-toe and giant steps with an explanation that refers to the relationship between the length of the step and the number of steps needed.

Game Time (page 101)

● Jacob; Pia; Lan; Jacob's game starts first.

■ Yuri—11:45 A.M.; Quinn—11:05 A.M.; Rick—11:35 A.M.

▲ Jessie—1:50 P.M.; Owen—12:50 P.M.; Lanie—3:25 P.M.; hands for each clock should be drawn correctly

Tell a Story (page 103)

Answers will vary.

Leo's Days (page 105)

● 11:30 A.M.; 3:10 P.M.; 3:30 P.M.

■ 7:15 A.M.; 9:15 A.M.; 1:45 P.M.; 3:55 P.M.

▲ 7:10 A.M.; 11:55 A.M.; 2:35 P.M.; 3:35 P.M.; 7:50 P.M.

Coin Combos (page 107)

● 2 dimes, 2 nickels, 1 penny

■ 1 quarter, 1 dime, and 5 pennies

▲ three of the four collections should be identified: 2 dimes, 1 nickel, and 5 pennies; 1 dime, 3 nickels, and 5 pennies; 1 dime, 2 nickels, and 10 pennies; or 1 dime, 1 nickel, and 15 pennies

Joke Sale (page 109)

● 1 dime and 1 nickel should be circled

■ 31¢

▲ 5¢

All My Coins (page 111)

● 80¢; penny

■ 53¢; 2 nickels and 3 pennies and 1 nickel and 8 pennies

▲ 92¢

Money Matters (page 113)

● $1.25

■ Luke; $1.01

▲ $1.05; 4 quarters and 1 nickel

What Shape Is Next? (page 115)

● △; triangle; patterns will vary

■ quadrilateral (or rhombus); patterns will vary

▲ hexagon; patterns will vary

Answer Key *(cont.)*

What Shape Am I? (page 117)

- ● triangle
- ■ quadrilateral (or rectangle)
- ▲ pentagon

Triangles and Squares (page 119)

- ● 8 triangles
- ■ 16 triangles
- ▲ 6 triangles

Dot Squares (page 121)

- ● 7 squares
- ■ 13 squares
- ▲ 20 squares

Shape Symbols (page 123)

- ● B
- ■ C
- ▲ A

How Many Cubes? (page 125)

- ● 8 cubes
- ■ 13 cubes
- ▲ 16 cubes

Make the Whole (page 127)

- ●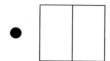
- ■
- ▲ 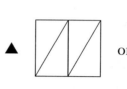 or

Find the Triangles (page 129)

- ● 5 triangles
- ■ 6 triangles
- ▲ 8 triangles

References Cited

Bright, G. W., and J. M. Joyner. 2005. *Dynamic classroom assessment: Linking mathematical understanding to instruction.* Chicago, IL: ETA Cuisenaire.

Brown, S. I., and M. I. Walter. 2005. *The art of problem posing.* Mahwah, NJ: Lawrence Earlbaum.

Cai, J. 2010. Helping elementary students become successful mathematical problem solvers. In *Teaching and learning mathematics: Translating research for elementary school teachers*, ed. D. V. Lambdin and F. K. Lester, Jr., 9–13. Reston, VA: NCTM.

D'Ambrosio, B. 2003. Teaching mathematics through problem solving: A historical perspective. In *Teaching mathematics through problem solving: Prekindergarten–Grade 6*, ed. F. K. Lester, Jr. and R. I. Charles, 37–50. Reston, VA: NCTM.

Goldenberg, E. P., N. Shteingold, and N. Feurzeig. 2003. Mathematical habits of mind for young children. In *Teaching mathematics through problem solving: Prekindergarten–Grade 6*, ed. F. K. Lester, Jr. and R. I. Charles, 51–61. Reston, VA: NCTM.

Michaels, S., C. O'Connor, and L. B. Resnick. 2008. Deliberative discourse idealized and realized: Accountable talk in the classroom and in civil life. *Studies in philosophy and education* 27 (4): 283–297.

National Center for Educational Statistics. 2010. Highlights from PISA 2009: Performance of U.S. 15-year-old students in reading, mathematics, and science literacy in an international context. http://nces.ed.gov/pubsearch/pubsinfo.asp?pubid=2011004.

National Governors Association Center for Best Practices and Council of Chief State School Officers. 2010. Common core state standards. http://www.corestandards.org/the-standards.

National Mathematics Advisory Panel. 2008. *Foundations for success: The final report of the National Mathematics Advisory Panel.* Washington, DC: U.S. Department of Education.

Polya, G. 1945. *How to solve it: A new aspect of mathematical method.* Princeton, NJ: Princeton University Press.

Sylwester, R. 2003. *A biological brain in a cultural classroom.* Thousand Oaks, CA: Corwin Press.

Tomlinson, C. A. 2003. *Fulfilling the promise of the differentiated classroom: Strategies and tools for responsive teaching.* Alexandria, VA: ASCD.

Vygotsky, L. 1986. *Thought and language.* Cambridge, MA: MIT Press.

Contents of the Teacher Resource CD

Teacher Resources

Page	Resource	Filename
27–29	Common Core State Standards Correlation	ccss.pdf
N/A	NCTM Standards Correlation	nctm.pdf
N/A	TESOL Standards Correlation	tesol.pdf
N/A	McREL Standards Correlation	mcrel.pdf
130	Student Response Form	studentresponse.pdf
131	Individual Observation Form	individualobs.pdf
132	Group Observation Form	groupobs.pdf
133	Record-Keeping Chart	recordkeeping.pdf
N/A	Exit Card Template	exitcard.pdf

Lesson Resource Pages

Page	Lesson	Filename
31	Who Is Who?	whoiswho.pdf
33	Design Blocks	designblocks.pdf
35	Yard Sale	yardsale.pdf
37	Equal Sums	equalsums.pdf
39	Venn Diagrams	venndiagrams.pdf
41	Books for Sale	booksforsale.pdf
43	Rubber Band Shapes	rubberband.pdf
45	Make a Face	makeface.pdf
47	Field Day	fieldday.pdf
49	Pose a Problem	poseaproblem.pdf
51	Bagfuls	bagfuls.pdf
53	Salad Garden	saladgarden.pdf
55	What Am I Thinking?	thinking.pdf
57	Same Sums	samesums.pdf
59	Puzzlers	puzzlers.pdf
61	Animal Stories	animal.pdf
63	Number Blocks	blocks.pdf
65	Figure It	figureit.pdf
67	Predict the Number	predict.pdf
69	Living on Main Street	mainstreet.pdf
71	Machine Math	machine.pdf
73	Show It	showit.pdf
75	Where Is It?	whereisit.pdf
77	Finish the Equations	finishequations.pdf
79	Ring Toss	ringtoss.pdf
81	Counting Along	countingalong.pdf

Contents of the Teacher Resource CD *(cont.)*

Lesson Resource Pages *(cont.)*

Page	Lesson	Filename
83	The Lee Family	leefamily.pdf
85	From the Beginning	fromthebeginning.pdf
87	All About Us	allaboutus.pdf
89	Last Names	lastnames.pdf
91	Measure It	measureit.pdf
93	Find the Lengths	findlengths.pdf
95	Lots of Ribbon	lotsribbon.pdf
97	Finish the Story	finishstory.pdf
99	Step-by-Step	stepbystep.pdf
101	Game Time	gametime.pdf
103	Tell a Story	tellstory.pdf
105	Leo's Days	leosdays.pdf
107	Coin Combos	coincombos.pdf
109	Joke Sale	jokesale.pdf
111	All My Coins	allmycoins.pdf
113	Money Matters	moneymatters.pdf
115	What Shape Is Next?	whatshapenext.pdf
117	What Shape Am I?	whatshape.pdf
119	Triangles and Squares	trianglessquares.pdf
121	Dot Squares	dotsquares.pdf
123	Shape Symbols	shapesymbols.pdf
125	How Many Cubes?	howmanycubes.pdf
127	Make the Whole	makewhole.pdf
129	Find the Triangles	findtriangles.pdf

Additional Lesson Resources

Page	Resource	Filename
36, 38	Number Cards	numbercards.pdf
74	Numberline 0–30	numberline30.pdf
74	Numberline 0–300	numberline300.pdf
78	Ring Toss Template	ringtosstemplate.pdf
104	Rosie's Times	rosiestimes.pdf
110	Coin Bar Graph	coingraph.pdf
120	Dot Paper Template	dotpaper.pdf
124	Building Blocks	buildingblocks.pdf

Notes

Notes

Notes

#50774—50 Leveled Math Problems, Level 2